Anonymus

Manual and Practical Instruction in Primary Schools

Final Report 1898

Anonymus

Manual and Practical Instruction in Primary Schools
Final Report 1898

ISBN/EAN: 9783742812704

Manufactured in Europe, USA, Canada, Australia, Japa

Cover: Foto ©Suzi / pixelio.de

Manufactured and distributed by brebook publishing software
(www.brebook.com)

Anonymus

Manual and Practical Instruction in Primary Schools

COMMISSION ON MANUAL AND PRACTICAL INSTRUCTION

IN

PRIMARY SCHOOLS UNDER THE BOARD OF NATIONAL EDUCATION

IN IRELAND.

FINAL REPORT

OF

THE COMMISSIONERS.

Presented to Parliament by Command of Her Majesty.

DUBLIN:

PRINTED FOR HER MAJESTY'S STATIONERY OFFICE,

BY ALEXANDER THOM & CO. (LIMITED).

And to be purchased, either directly or through any Bookseller, from

Hodges, Figgis, and Co. (Limited), 104, Grafton-street, Dublin; or

Eyre and Spottiswoode, East Harding-street, Fleet-street, E.C., and

32, Abingdon-street, Westminster, S.W.; or

John Menzies and Co., 12, Hanover-street, Edinburgh, and 90, West Nile-street, Glasgow.

1898.

TABLE OF CONTENTS.

WARRANT APPOINTING THE COMMISSION.

CHIEF SECRETARY'S OFFICE,
DUBLIN CASTLE.

BY THE LORD LIEUTENANT-GENERAL AND GENERAL GOVERNOR OF IRELAND.

CADOGAN.

WHEREAS it appears to Us to be expedient that a Commission should forthwith issue with a view to determining how far, and in what form, Manual and Practical instruction should be included in the Educational System of the Primary Schools under the Board of National Education in Ireland.

Now We, GEORGE HENRY, EARL CADOGAN, Lord Lieutenant-General and General Governor of Ireland, do hereby nominate and appoint—

SOMERSET RICHARD, Earl Belmore, G.C.M.G.;
His Grace the Most Reverend WILLIAM CONYNGHAM, Baron Plunket, D.D., LL.D.;
His Grace the Most Reverend WILLIAM J. WALSH, D.D.;
The Right Hon. CHRISTOPHER PALLES, LL.D., Lord Chief Baron;
The Right Hon. CHRISTOPHER TALBOT REDINGTON, M.A.;
His Honor Judge SHAW, M.A.;
The Right Reverend Monsignor MOLLOY, D.D., D.SC.;
The Reverend HENRY EVANS, D.D.;
The Reverend HAMILTON WILSON, D.D.;
Professor GEORGE F. FITZGERALD, F.T.C.D.;
STANLEY HARRINGTON, Esquire, B.A.;
WILLIAM ROBERT J. MOLLOY, Esquire;
Captain T. B. SHAW, late Royal Engineers, Inspector of Science and Art Schools under the Science and Art Department in England; and
J. STRUTHERS, Esquire, Inspector of Schools under the Scotch Education Department,

to be Our Commissioners for the purpose aforesaid; that is to say to inquire and report with a view to determining how far, and in what form, manual and practical instruction should be included in the Educational System of the Primary Schools under the Board of National Education in Ireland.

And for the better effecting the purposes of this Our Commission, We do by these presents authorize and empower you the aforesaid Commissioners, or any three or more of you to be named by you, to call before you, or any three or more of you, such persons as you may think fit to examine, and by whom you may be the better informed in the matter hereby submitted for your consideration, and everything connected therewith, and generally to inquire of and concerning the premises by all other lawful ways and means whatsoever.

And also to call for and examine such books, documents, papers, writings, or records as you or any three or more of you as aforesaid shall think useful for the purposes of the Inquiry.

And We also by these presents authorize and empower you, or any three or more of you as aforesaid, to visit and personally inspect such places as you, or any three or more of you, may deem expedient for the purposes aforesaid, and also to employ such persons as you may think fit to assist you in undertaking any inquiry for the purposes aforesaid as you may deem expedient to make, and Our pleasure is that you, or any three or more of you as aforesaid, do from time to time and with all convenient speed report to Us what you shall find concerning the premises.

And We further by these presents ordain that this Our Commission shall continue in full force and virtue, and that you Our Commissioners do from time to time proceed in the execution thereof, although the same be not continued from time to time by adjournment.

And for your further assistance in the execution of these presents, We do hereby appoint JAMES DERMOT DALY, Esquire, M.A., to be the Secretary to this Our Commission, whose services and assistance We require you to use from time to time as occasion may require.

Given at Her Majesty's Castle of Dublin, this 25th day of January, 1897.

COMMISSION ON MANUAL AND PRACTICAL INSTRUCTION

IN

PRIMARY SCHOOLS UNDER THE BOARD OF NATIONAL EDUCATION IN IRELAND.

FINAL REPORT.

TO HIS EXCELLENCY GEORGE HENRY, EARL CADOGAN, K.G.,

&c., &c., &c.,

LORD LIEUTENANT-GENERAL AND GENERAL GOVERNOR OF IRELAND.

MAY IT PLEASE YOUR EXCELLENCY,

We the Commissioners appointed "to inquire and report with a view to determining how far, and in what form, Manual and Practical Instruction should be included in the Educational System of Primary Schools under the Board of National Education in Ireland," beg to submit to your Excellency our Fourth and final Report, on the subject of our inquiry.

In carrying out the task imposed upon us by your Excellency's Commission of January 25, 1897, we have had ninety-three meetings, of which fifty-seven were sittings for the receiving of evidence. We have taken the evidence of 186 persons whom we considered qualified to give information on the matters submitted to us, and we have visited 119 schools, in most of which we have had an opportunity of

Proceedings of the Commission.

In the last days of September, and during the early part of October, we made a tour through Ireland, visiting schools and taking evidence in Kilkenny, Waterford, Lismore, Cork, Limerick, Galway, Sligo, Belfast, and Londonderry. At Waterford, we took the opportunity of inspecting the "De la Salle" Training College; and during our visit to Cork, we inspected the Munster Dairy Farm, in the neighbourhood of that city. From Ireland we passed over to Scotland, and during the latter part of October, we visited schools and took evidence at Dumfries, Lockerbie, Edinburgh, Leith, Glasgow, and Dundee.

Since our return from Scotland we have held many sittings in Dublin, for the taking of evidence and the preparation of our Report. We have also visited the Albert Model Farm at Glasnevin, the Training College in Marlborough-street, "St. Patrick's" Training College, the "Church of Ireland" Training College, and "Our Lady of Mercy" Training College. The evidence taken in September, October, November, and December, is presented as a supplement to this Report.

With a view to ascertain the existing facts with regard to Manual and Practical Instruction in Germany, France, Switzerland, and Holland, we employed as our assistants to visit those countries, Messrs. Purser, Rolleston, Bonaparte Wyse, and Hughes-Dowling. The reports of these gentlemen will be found in Appendix B. We have had the advantage, too, of the assistance of Mr. M. E. Sadler, Director of Special Inquiries and Reports to the Committee of Council on Education, who was kind enough to furnish us with a memorandum on Manual Training for boys in Primary Schools in foreign countries.[1] For our information regarding schools in the United States, we are indebted to the very complete and exhaustive Reports issued by the United States Bureau of Education. We have also had the benefit of the experience of one of our colleagues, Professor Fitzgerald, who took the occasion of a visit to America, in the autumn of last year, to see some of the primary schools in that country.

Result of Inquiry.

After careful consideration of the evidence laid before us, and of the facts which we have seen for ourselves, we now proceed to report, in accordance with your Excellency's Commission, how far, and in what form, Manual and Practical Instruction should be included in the system of primary education carried out by the National Education Board in Ireland. We may at once express our strong conviction that Manual and Practical Instruction ought to be introduced, as far as possible, into all schools where it does not at present exist, and that, in those schools where it does exist, it ought to be largely developed and extended. We are satisfied that such a change will not involve any detriment to the literary education of the pupils, while it will contribute largely to develop their faculties, to quicken their intelligence, and to fit them better for their work in life.

Report divided into three parts.

It will be convenient, we think, for your Excellency, if, at the outset of our Report, we set forth, in a summary way, the general conclusions at which we have arrived on this subject, and the main grounds on which these conclusions are based. We will afterwards deal more in particular with the various branches of Manual and Practical Instruction, showing, with respect to each branch, what is the present condition of primary education in Ireland, and explaining in detail the changes which we propose should be made. Lastly, we shall briefly point out certain changes in other parts of the system of National Education, which will become necessary, as we think, with a view to the development of Manual and Practical Instruction.

PART I.

GENERAL CONCLUSIONS, AND THE GROUNDS ON WHICH THEY ARE BASED.

Part I. — General Conclusions.

1. KINDERGARTEN.—We are of opinion that the general principles and methods of the system known by the name of Kindergarten, which have been already introduced into some of the schools under the National Education Board, should be extended as far as possible to all schools attended by infant children.

carrying on the manual training of the children, from the Kindergarten stage to the higher grades of Manual Instruction. Further we consider that some form of more advanced Manual Instruction should be introduced, as far as possible, in the higher classes of schools for boys; and we recommend, as most suitable for this purpose, instruction in the principles and practice of Woodwork, treated educationally. The object to be aimed at, is not to make the boys carpenters, but to train them in habits of accurate observation, careful measurement, and exact workmanship. Such habits we regard as of great value to all boys, whatever may be their subsequent career in life.

Part I. — General Conclusions.

III. DRAWING.—We recommend that Drawing should be made compulsory, as far as possible, in all National Schools. The first elements of it find a place in the Kindergarten system, and it should be continued, we think, to the end of the school career. In the classes above the Kindergarten, it should be associated with Hand and Eye Training, with Woodwork, and to some extent also with Elementary Science, as soon as these subjects are introduced.

IV. ELEMENTARY SCIENCE.—We are of opinion that a simple course of Elementary Science should form a part of ordinary education in National Schools. This course should be so framed as to bring home to the minds of the children an intelligent knowledge of the common facts of nature, and the rudimentary principles of science. In the lower classes, it should consist in great part of object lessons; and in the higher classes, it should be illustrated by simple experiments. The pupils should be encouraged and assisted, as far as may be found practicable, to take part in the experiments. The programme for this course, while following everywhere the same general lines, may with advantage be varied in its details, according to the circumstances of the locality, and the character and condition of the children.

V. AGRICULTURE.—We do not think that Agriculture as an art, that is to say practical farming, is a subject that properly belongs to elementary education. At present, the study of what is called the Theory of Agriculture, is compulsory for boys in all rural schools, and is highly encouraged by fees. But our inquiry has shown that this study consists, for the most part, in committing a text-book to memory; and we have come to the conclusion that it has little educational or practical value. We recommend instead, that the course of Elementary Science to be taught in rural schools, should be so framed as to illustrate the more simple scientific principles that underlie the art and industry of Agriculture. We also recommend the maintenance and extension of School Gardens, as a means by which these scientific principles may be illustrated and made interesting to the pupils. On the other hand, we do not consider that the maintenance of School Farms, the object of which is to teach the art of Agriculture, properly belongs to the functions of a Board of primary education. As regards the Model Farm at Glasnevin, and the Munster Dairy School, we think that they could be made more useful for the purposes of agricultural education, if placed in charge of an Agricultural Department, whenever such a Department is established in Ireland.

VI. COOKERY, LAUNDRY WORK, AND DOMESTIC SCIENCE.—We think it very desirable that Cookery, Laundry Work, and Domestic Science, should be taught, as far as may be found practicable, in girls schools. We cannot advise that these subjects should, at present, be made compulsory; but we do recommend that aid should be freely given to provide the necessary buildings and equipment for teaching them; and that managers and teachers should be encouraged to take them up, by a liberal system of grants.

VII. NEEDLEWORK.—Needlework should continue to form, as at present, an important element in all schools for girls. The first elements of it are taught in the Kindergarten system. It should be continued in Classes I., II., and III., as a part of Hand and Eye Training; and, in the higher classes, advanced Needlework will naturally occupy the time devoted to Woodwork in schools for boys.

(f) DRILL AND PHYSICAL EXERCISES.—Various kinds of Drill and Physical Exercises are now a recognised part of primary education in England, in Scotland, and on the Continent of Europe; and we think they should be introduced into the primary schools of Ireland, with the least possible delay. We are satisfied, from what we have seen and heard on this subject, that such exercises contribute largely to the health, the spirits, and the general well-being of the children. They are no additional burden on school life, but rather a pleasant form of recreation; and the children return from them to their studies with renewed energy.

It will be for the Commissioners of National Education to consider and determine in what manner these various changes can best be introduced into their system. But we have ventured to make some general suggestions on this head, which it may be well to set forth here in a summary form.

We think that the changes recommended ought to be introduced, not all at once, but gradually and tentatively. They should be tried first in the larger centres, and afterwards extended to more remote districts. It would be necessary, at the outset, to engage the services of experts, from outside the present staff of the National Education Board, whose duty it would be to organise the classes, and to aid the teachers with their counsel and instruction. But we have no doubt that this work, after a little time, could be taken up by the ordinary staff of the Board. Again, it is extremely important that all future teachers should be trained in the new subjects; and the programme of the Training Colleges must accordingly be framed to this end, with as little delay as possible.

We have carefully considered the question, by what means time may be found for the several exercises in manual and practical training which we have recommended; and we have pointed out certain modifications in the present programme of studies, which may be adopted for that purpose, and which, we believe, will not interfere unfavourably with the course of instruction hitherto given in the National Schools.

Lastly, we are strongly of opinion that the system of Results Fees, depending on the individual examination of pupils, at present in force in the National Schools, ought not to be applied to these subjects of Manual and Practical Instruction. While it should be always open to the Inspector to examine individual pupils, we think that the grants awarded to the teacher, in these subjects, should largely depend on the general evidence of his own zeal and industry, on the efficiency of his method of teaching, and on his power to arouse and hold the attention of his class.

The considerations by which we have been led to the general conclusions above set out, will be fully discussed in the second part of this Report, under the several heads of Manual and Practical Instruction. But we think it will be for your Excellency's convenience, that the general summary of our conclusions should be here followed by a general summary of the grounds on which they are based.

I. First, then, there are reasons founded on educational principles. The present system, which consists largely in the study of books, is one-sided in its character; and it leaves some of the most useful faculties of the mind absolutely untrained. We think it important that children should be taught not merely to take in knowledge from books, but to observe with intelligence the material world around them; that they should be trained in habits of correct reasoning on the facts observed; and that they should, even at school, acquire some skill in the use of hand and eye to execute the conceptions of the brain. Such a training we regard as valuable to all, but especially valuable to those whose lives are to be mainly devoted to industrial arts and occupations. The great bulk of the pupils attending primary schools under the National Board will have to earn their bread by the work of their hands; it is therefore important that they should be trained, from the beginning, to use their hands with dexterity and intelligence.[1]

[1] The general educational value of Manual Training in primary schools, especially for those who have to devote their lives to manual work, has been insisted on by a great number of witnesses. The following may be taken as examples:—Mr. J. W. [illegible], Director of Manual Training to the Birmingham School Board, vol. ii., qq. [illegible]; Mr. George H. [illegible], Head Master, Board School, Birmingham, vol. ii., qq. [illegible]; Sir Philip Magnus, Director and Secretary of [illegible] Institute, vol. ii., qq. [illegible]; Mr. T. G. Rooper, H.M. Inspector of Schools in England, vol. ii., qq. [illegible]; Mr. [illegible], Organiser of Manual Instruction to the London School Board, vol. ii., qq. [illegible]; Mr. [illegible], Instructor in Woodwork to the [illegible] School Board, vol. ii., qq. [illegible]; Mr. Arnold Graves, Honorary Secretary to the Technical Education Association for Ireland, vol. iii., q. [illegible]; Mr. [illegible], Head Master, [illegible] Public School, Edinburgh, vol. iv., qq. [illegible]; Mr. J. G. Kerr, Head Master, Allan Glen's School, Glasgow, vol. iv., qq. [illegible].

f those schools in
a system as we

III. Lastly, there is a consideration of a practical character, which seems to us deserving of no little weight. A strong desire exists throughout this country, and it is growing stronger every day, for the introduction of a general system of Technical Education. It is thought that a good system of Technical Education would contribute largely towards the development of arts and industries in Ireland; and in this opinion we entirely concur. But the present system of primary education is so one-sided in its character that it leaves the pupils quite unprepared for Technical Education. The clever boys trained in the National Schools, if they are disposed to seek for a higher education, may pass with advantage into Intermediate Schools of the kind now general in Ireland; but they are not fit to enter a Technical School, even if they had such a school at their doors. Now it seems to us that the changes we recommend would go far to remedy this defect. The system of National Education, modified as we propose, would give an all-round training to the faculties of the children, and would thus lay a solid foundation for any system of higher education—literary, scientific, or technical—which might afterwards be found suitable to their talents and their circumstances.

PART II.

REPORT IN DETAIL ON THE VARIOUS BRANCHES OF MANUAL AND PRACTICAL INSTRUCTION.

Having thus laid before your Excellency a short summary of the general conclusions at which we have arrived, and of the grounds on which they are based, we will now go on to discuss, more in particular, the several branches of Manual and Practical Instruction which have formed the subject of our inquiry. In dealing with each branch, we will first state how far it finds a place at present in the primary schools of Ireland. We will then consider, at some length, the various questions that may arise in connection with it, referring as we proceed to the evidence we have taken, to the views and opinions of experts which have been submitted to us, and to the schools which we ourselves have seen. Lastly, we will set out, in distinct form, the specific recommendations that we make, with respect to its introduction or development in the educational system of the National Schools.

It is to be regretted that in Ireland, as elsewhere, the word Kindergarten is frequently used in a very misleading way. Not uncommonly the expression may be heard that Kindergarten is taught, or is not taught, in a certain school, as if Kindergarten were a subject to be taught to children, like reading, writing, and other subjects of the school programme. In the narrow and erroneous view implied in this use of the word, Kindergarten seems to be identified with the exercises, somewhat in the nature of children's games, which the children under Kindergarten instruction are taught to go through. This narrow and misleading view of the subject cannot but create a prejudice against the Kindergarten system in the minds of many teachers, and hinder its introduction into many schools, especially schools conducted by male teachers. Part II. Section I. Kindergarten. Use of the word Kindergarten.

It may not be amiss here to refer to the original conception of the Kindergarten and its work, as devised by Froebel, the author of the system. Froebel's Kindergarten.

The term Kindergarten as used by Froebel has no reference to any subject of instruction. It designates a method, formulated by him, for the education of children in their early years. Then, in a secondary sense, the word naturally came to designate the institution or place in which children are educated according to that method.

The method of education formulated by Froebel is based upon certain fundamental principles, fully, but somewhat diffusely, expounded by him in a number of his writings. But in its working, this method admits of endless variety in points of detail. Variety in detail is, in fact, one of its essential features, for the process should always be adapted to the capacity of the individual child.

The leading principles embodied in the Kindergarten method of education may be stated as follows:—(1) That education means the development of all the powers of the child; (2) that, in the process of education, the development of the bodily, as well as of the mental, faculties is to be aimed at; (3) that education is essentially defective if it fails to cultivate the moral sense; (4) that what is spontaneous in the child is the really valuable part of the process of education, so that the aim of the teacher should be, not so much to give the child instruction ab extra, as to supply materials and opportunities for the mind of the child itself to work upon; (5) that these materials and opportunities should be supplied in a well-considered harmonious order, each step in the process of education being naturally led up to by what preceded it; (6) that, as far as possible, the process should be adapted to the disposition, capacity, and actual development of each individual child.

Even from this brief general statement it will be seen how misleading is the view in which the Kindergarten method is regarded as a system of mere childish amusements. The real value of Kindergarten work is that it draws out the natural powers of the child, training and strengthening, by suitable exercise, those faculties by which knowledge is afterwards to be acquired, and the work of life is to be done.

The German name Kindergarten (Kinder, children; Garten, garden) given to this system by Froebel, admirably expresses its spirit. The name is sometimes taken as if it primarily signified the place in which this method of teaching is to be carried on, and indicated it as a garden. In the view more generally taken, however, the name by which Froebel wished his system to be known is of far deeper significance. Gardens have indeed an important place in the working of the system. But the "garden" which Froebel wished the name Kindergarten to suggest, is a metaphorical one; it is the teacher's sphere of work, and the plants to be tended in it are the children.

The name, thus understood, is aptly chosen to bring into prominence the distinctive feature of the system which Froebel intended it to designate. A gardener does not furnish the plants in his garden with leaves and fruit, brought from without, to be attached to them by any artificial process. He tends the plants with care; he helps them in their growth by supplying them with every aid that his skill can suggest as best calculated to promote the free exercise of their own vitality; he removes from about them everything that could harm them, or check their natural development. Precisely similar should be the work of the teacher charged with the education of children, more especially in their earlier years. They are tender plants, and the Kindergarten teacher is the gardener.

The general lines on which Kindergarten teaching is worked out—all of them based upon a close and sympathetic study of the ways and capabilities of children—are fully described in numerous works on the subject. It is sufficient here to mention the large part assigned in the system to singing, and to organised games of various kinds; the use made in it of natural objects, and of the phenomena of nature, as means of education even in the most elementary stages; and its employment of a number of small, easily-handled objects of simple geometrical form, such as balls, and cubes, and cylinders, termed "Gifts," which are intended to awaken and direct a spirit of inquiry in the child,

Part II. Section I. Recommendations. Froebel's Kindergarten.

and of a number of simple manual exercises, termed "Occupations," which represent the first steps in the training of both hand and eye.

The spirit of the Kindergarten is sympathetically described in the following words of the late Sir Patrick Keenan:—"The most innocent, the most hopeful portion of all educational life, with its school appliances lovingly called 'gifts,' and its school exercises fittingly called 'plays'; no set tasks intrude, no hard lessons chill. Spontaneously the faculties dawn, the affections ripen, the senses quicken."[1] He regards the Kindergarten as "a pleasant initiation to what is still popularly called the drudgery of school life."

It is essential to keep in view that in Froebel's plan, Kindergarten teaching is a thing altogether apart from school-work. It should begin at home, when the child is but a few months old, the mother being the first teacher. When about three years old, the child begins to attend the place of regularly organised Kindergarten teaching,—we must not speak of it as a school,—where the system is carried out by a skilled teacher. Kindergarten teaching should thus cover the entire period from the first dawn of intelligence in the child up to the close of the sixth or seventh year of age. During that period, nothing in the nature of formal instruction, even of the most elementary character, in reading, writing, or any other such school subject should be attempted; all such instruction should be reserved for the school, as distinct from the Kindergarten, and the children should not go to school until they are at least six or seven years old. By those who have adopted Froebel's ideas in their integrity it is maintained that much more rapid progress is made in the various branches of school-work, when the children bring to them faculties quickened and quickened by the Kindergarten discipline of the Kindergarten.

Misconceptions.

Before proceeding to state in detail our recommendations under this head, we think it useful to make some observations in reference especially to two particular points in the Kindergarten system, as to which there is reason to apprehend that the essential nature of the system is not always properly understood.

We may, we fear, to a large extent apply to Ireland what a recent writer on Kindergarten teaching has said of England:—

"The educational public are still inclined to regard a long list of games and occupations as the chief addition which Friedrich Froebel has made to the sum of educational [illegible]. Doubtless a few of his leading theories have been expounded in our language, but they do not as yet exert practical influence on the organisation of Kindergartens and Infant Schools. Theory and practice stand aloof from one another. Popular notions commonly connected with the English 'Kindergarten' have [illegible]. To many the [illegible] . . . Manuals on the occupations . . . are apt to [illegible] the children's time, because they prescribe an amount of mechanical work, not in connection with the educational purpose [illegible] . . . The Kindergarten has, indeed, degenerated, even in the country of its origin (Germany), into a place where children are pleasantly amused, folding paper, playing games, &c.; and English people may be excused if misconceptions concerning the aim and object of the institution are still frequent amongst them."[2]

The "Gifts" and "Occupations."

In our statement of the points that stand prominently forward in Kindergarten teaching, we have referred to the materials and opportunities with which to provide the children as a means of developing their natural powers. Amongst these are the "Gifts" and the "Occupations," already mentioned. The Gifts and the Occupations were most carefully planned by Froebel, each for a specific purpose, and their respective parts in the working of the system, when it is in the hands of a teacher who has really grasped its principles and is imbued with its spirit, are of high educational value. Through their use, under the direction of a competent teacher, habits of observation are gradually formed; the first lessons in the importance of accuracy, even in matters of apparently trifling detail, are unconsciously learned; an intelligent interest in many external objects is awakened; the sense of symmetry and the sense of form are cultivated; and the constructive powers of the child are intelligently directed and developed.

But in the working of the system it is easy to give undue prominence to the Gifts and Occupations; and the tendency of unskilful teachers to do so, and even, from a total misconception of the purpose of these Gifts and Occupations, to reduce the whole system of Kindergarten teaching to a mere instruction of the children in the working out of a set of prescribed exercises, has to be carefully guarded against. The Gifts and Occupations are merely the means, or rather they are but some of the means, which the teacher is

[1] Address delivered before the Social Science Congress, Dublin, 5th October, 1881, page 6.

[2] The Kindergarten Principle; its Educational Value and Chief Applications, by M. J. Lyschinska, Superintendent of Method in Infant Schools under the School Board of London [illegible], London, 1880, pages 1-3.

to employ, in leading the child to begin to think for itself, act for itself, and rely upon itself, and yet at the same time to subordinate its own individual interests to those of the little community of which it is a member. They afford opportunity for exercises in construction, and, to a certain extent, exercises in design, to be worked out by the children. But the Kindergarten system is sadly misapplied when this portion of it is perverted into a mechanical reproduction of set exercises. The mere reproduction of anything is inconsistent with the fundamental principles of the system; children exercise little thought in merely copying what is put before them. So-called Kindergarten work done on such a line, is not, in any true sense of the word, Kindergarten work at all. And not only does it deprive the children of practically all the advantages of good Kindergarten teaching, but it gives rise to a prejudice against the system, which very naturally obstructs the introduction of it into the schools.

Part II. Section I. Kindergarten.

Again, it seems to be very frequently overlooked that, in Froebel's ideas, one of the most prominent features of Kindergarten teaching is the use which should be made of natural objects and of natural phenomena, as a means of education even in its earliest stages. A garden, or plot of ground, is a leading feature of the method of education formulated by Froebel. He attached the utmost importance to having the children brought directly into contact with nature. He did so, not only because this afforded an easy means of laying the groundwork of a sound method of instruction in natural science, but also because, to use his own phrase, "from every object in nature there is a way to God." It was also a principle of his that children are born with a great capacity for the enjoyment of the sights and sounds and changes which nature so abundantly displays. The child's sympathy with flowers and birds and animals should be fostered and directed. And it must never be forgotten that in all this, the important point is, not that the children should be merely talked to about these objects, or encouraged themselves to talk about them, but that they should be in contact with them, and be occupied with them. As it has been well expressed by the writer on the Kindergarten principle from whom we have already quoted, it is not the dry mastery of the facts of nature, but the personal relation in which the children find themselves to natural objects, that awakens their interest in the observation of nature and of natural phenomena, and makes this available as a means of education.[1] If this use of the objects and of the facts of nature as a means of education be lost out of sight in Kindergarten teaching, "the whole organisation lacks a life-giving principle; its parts have but an accidental and loose connexion; the occupations and gifts are not linked together by any vivifying thought."[2]

Natural Objects and Phenomena.

The Kindergarten system in its integrity, as it was conceived by Froebel, and as it has been carried out in many places in Germany and elsewhere, has never been adopted as a part of the system of National Education in Ireland, or of the corresponding systems of elementary education in England and Scotland. This would seem to be sufficiently accounted for by two leading features of the Kindergarten method as thus understood: (1) the exclusion from its scheme of work of all instruction, even in those subjects of elementary education, reading, writing, and arithmetic, commonly known as the "three R's"; and (2) the individual character of its teaching, with the consequent necessity for the employment of a very large staff of teachers in proportion to the number of pupils. In other countries also, and probably for the same reason, it would seem to be generally recognised that in the matter of education the work of the State begins only with the school.

Kindergarten and the School.

But although the Kindergarten, in the full and original sense of the word, has not found a place in the school system either of Ireland, or of England or Scotland, the work of the Infants School has, in Ireland to a certain extent, and to a much greater extent in England and in Scotland, been brought within the influence of Kindergarten ideas. The evidence which we have received as to the beneficial results of this influence upon the schools is emphatic and conclusive.[3]

In Infants Schools and classes the original idea too often was to instruct young children as rapidly as possible in the elements of reading, writing, and arithmetic; and

---

[1] The Kindergarten Principle (Lyschinska), London, 1880, p. 66.
[2] Ibid., page [illegible].
[3] Evid., vol. ii., [illegible]

Part II. Section I. Kindergarten.

it is to be regretted that in many cases this object is the one still aimed at. In a school worked on such a principle attention is practically confined to this one object, and any time that is given to occupations designed to train or develop the natural instincts of the children is apt to be regarded as so much time wasted. But it has been found by experience that when the work of these schools is modified by the liberal introduction of ideas borrowed from the Kindergarten, more scope is given to the energies of the children, an interest in the instruction which they receive is awakened, their faculty of sustained attention is sharpened, and their whole school life is made brighter and happier. There is overwhelming testimony to show that all this is done without retarding their proficiency in the "three R's," but rather with the result of advancing it.

Value of Kindergarten teaching.

The following opinion of Sir Joshua Fitch represents the general scope of the evidence received by us on this point in England and Scotland:—"All experience shows that if the teaching of the elements of reading, writing, drawing, and counting, are judiciously alternated with the playful Froebelian exercises, the children make in the long run better progress, even in the elements of instruction, than heretofore."[1]

Mr. Rooper, one of Her Majesty's Inspectors of Schools in England, gives similar testimony:—"There is," he says, "no question about the value of the Kindergarten occupations for the younger children; they have been introduced practically in all infant schools in England, and especially in the large towns. . . . I find that all the teachers, managers, and inspectors are amply satisfied with the results. I have never come across any teacher in any infant school who, having once adopted the Kindergarten occupations, has any desire to go back to the time when there were no such occupations, and when the whole time was spent over reading, writing, and arithmetic."[2]

Another of Her Majesty's Inspectors, Mr. [illegible], speaking especially for the Cumberland district, including the Counties of Cumberland and Westmorland, in which there are many small rural schools, bears very decided testimony to the advantages resulting from the introduction of Kindergarten teaching. "The system of Kindergarten," he says, "has been introduced since I first began my work as inspector, and I can certainly speak very highly of the effect it has had, both in training teachers, and in developing intelligence; and in giving the relaxation which was very much needed. The intermixture of Kindergarten with the ordinary work, reading, writing, and arithmetic, is the best system possible."[3]

Recommendations.

Accordingly, whilst, in view of what has been done in other countries, we do not venture to recommend the introduction of Kindergarten teaching, pure and simple, as a part of the system of National Education in Ireland, we think it of the utmost importance that all infant instruction, whether in separate Infants Schools, or in the infants classes of other National Schools, should be permeated by the Kindergarten spirit, and that the recognised methods of Kindergarten teaching should as far as possible be adopted.

We are of opinion too that the Kindergarten principles and methods have an important bearing, not merely on the work in the Infants Schools and classes, but on all the work of the school.

National Schools generally.

As regards the National Schools generally, we recommend that the instruction of infants,—that is, roughly speaking, of children under seven years of age,—should approximate as nearly to the Kindergarten ideal as the circumstances of the case will permit. This approximation can, of course, more easily be effected in schools where the children under seven are sufficiently numerous to form a class, or a department, by themselves, under the charge of a special teacher or special staff of teachers. In such cases, we are decidedly of opinion that the education of these children, so far from consisting exclusively of instruction in the "three R's," should never begin with such instruction, but should, at first, be of a purely Kindergarten character, and should continue throughout to consist largely of Kindergarten exercises.

We make this recommendation not alone on the general grounds already stated, but also for the special reason that we think it important that teachers should realise, from the very beginning of a child's education, that education, in the true sense of the word, is at once broader and deeper than mere formal instruction in the "Three R's," and that such instruction is only one—though, no doubt, a very important one—of the many possible instruments of education. It cannot be too strongly emphasised that the

[1] Evid., vol. ii., 6465.
[2] Evid., vol. ii., 3031.
[3] Evid., vol. iii., 4324.

function of Kindergarten exercises in Infants School education is not merely to provide an agreeable relief to severe but more important studies, but to be real factors in the all-round education of the child.

We do not think it possible to lay down a hard and fast rule as to the age when instruction in the "Three R's" should begin. Much depends on the manner in which such instruction is given, but we consider, on the one hand, that some introduction of the elements of reading, writing, and arithmetic is not necessarily incompatible with a detailed adherence to Kindergarten principles, and, on the other hand, that the omission, or partial omission, of these subjects in the education of children at or under six years of age need not retard their subsequent progress in them.

In the foregoing recommendations we have had mainly in view the case of schools where the infants are sufficiently numerous to justify the setting aside of a teacher or teachers for them alone. But the recommendations apply with scarcely less force to the numerous cases where there is but one teacher for the infants and for Classes I. and II.

In Ireland, however, there are many schools in which one teacher has to teach all the classes, from the Infants Class up to Class VI. In such circumstances it is not to be expected that the Kindergarten programme should be followed in all its fulness in the instruction of the infants and younger children; the benefit to be derived in these cases from an intelligent study of Kindergarten ideas on the part of the teacher is to be looked for in the applicability of those ideas to the work of the school as a whole, rather than to the special work of the Infants and other lower classes. This does not at all imply that the interests of the younger children should be overlooked, or should even be subordinated to that of the more advanced pupils. It seems to us that but little profit can result to very young children from spending a long day in school if they are simply left to their own devices, while the teacher concentrates his attention on the higher classes. Definite work for a much shorter school day would be in every way more profitable to the younger children, provided that it were guided by an enlightened understanding of their needs and capabilities. In the time set free by the earlier dismissal of the younger classes the teacher would be able to give his undistracted attention to the work of the more advanced pupils. These pupils, on the other hand, might, not merely without loss, but rather with profit, devote to some independent work, specially laid out for them, the time during which the teacher is occupied with the younger children. With the view of facilitating such a distribution of the teacher's efforts in the case of small schools, we suggest it as well worthy of the consideration of the Board of National Education whether in the case of a school with only one teacher, the rule by which infants may be dismissed early might not with advantage be extended to some others of the junior classes.

We do not think that it is within our province, or that it would serve any useful purpose, to describe in detail the proper methods of conducting an Infants School on Kindergarten principles. It is obviously to be desired that the management of these schools should eventually pass into the hands of teachers adequately trained in the methods of the Kindergarten and fully imbued with its spirit. With this end in view, we again refer to this subject in the section on Training Colleges, in the third part of our Report. No part of a teacher's preparation is less a matter of reading or instruction, or is more a matter of prolonged and thoughtful training, than the preparation for the charge of infants. And we cannot too strongly express our conviction of the injudiciousness of the somewhat prevalent practice of relegating the instruction of infants to the charge of monitors or other imperfectly trained teachers. On the other hand we think it possible that monitors and pupil-teachers may render useful assistance in an Infants School when acting under the direction of a capable mistress, and may themselves at the same time receive the best of all preparations for their future work.

So far, we have dealt with Kindergarten methods as applied in the teaching of the infants and other younger children, but, as we have already indicated, Kindergarten ideas are of value quite outside the range of that special department of school-work. In connexion with the subjects of our inquiry, the applicability of these methods to the school-work of older children is even more important. We consider that the idea of education embodied in the Kindergarten system is one to be kept in view at all stages of school life, and that therefore a study of its principles and some knowledge of its methods should be regarded as indispensable elements in the training of all teachers, males as well as females, even though they should never have occasion to teach an Infants class.

Part II. Section 2. Kindergarten.

All the methods of the Kindergarten converge on one supreme object, the education of the child, or in other words, the development of all the faculties of the child in an orderly and harmonious fashion. The activities of the Kindergarten, therefore, range over a wide field. A child naturally seeks scope for its instinct of symmetry, its love of nature, its delight in rhythm and movement, its inquisitiveness, its desire to create. The exercises of the Kindergarten have regard to all these instincts, and, whilst providing for their legitimate gratification, turn them to educational account. It is in this way that the several characteristic features of the Kindergarten have their origin—the imitative games, with their sympathetic representation of natural incidents; the singing; the story-telling; the tending of plants and the loving care of pets; the "Gifts" presented to the children, which they examine with natural curiosity, and in doing so, acquire certain fundamental conceptions of form and number; and the "Occupations" which provide them with material for the exercise of their growing power of construction. The exercises of the Kindergarten, combined, as they are, with due regard to proper sequence and proportion, constitute a complete and well-reasoned scheme of education for younger children. We would point out that the conduct of school-work for older children may advantageously be influenced by the same considerations.

We realise that after the age of seven, instruction in the "three R's," must form the staple of school-work; but it cannot be seriously contended that these subjects alone, even with the addition of grammar and geography, provide adequate exercise for the faculties of a child, or that the restriction of the work of the school to this comparatively limited and often uncongenial field of effort is calculated to produce a feeling of joy and satisfaction in school life. Nor do we agree with those who think that undisciplined play out of school hours, or, what is still commoner, aimless idleness, is any adequate substitute for the corresponding activities of the Kindergarten. We dissent even more strongly from the view that work which a child may do, whether on the farm, or in the factory, or at casual occupations, may be regarded as an equivalent for educational manual exercises in the school.

The Kindergarten idea applied to school-work generally.

On the ground, then, no less of general educational principle than of practical utility, we shall, in the following portions of our Report, make certain recommendations as to the manner in which we think the various Kindergarten exercises may be continued and developed in the classes for older children. These recommendations will be found in the sections on Educational Handwork, on Drawing, and on Elementary Science: all of these we regard, educationally speaking, as developments of different sides of Kindergarten work, and therefore essential elements in any system of education for older children which is to approximate to the Kindergarten ideal of completeness. Manual exercises for hand and eye training, followed by woodwork or some other form of Sloyd teaching, are, or should be, the logical development of specific Kindergarten Occupations; Drawing is the continuation of another; Elementary Science, in method no less than in subject matter, is a development of the child's dealings with nature in the Kindergarten.

We have thought it right to direct special attention to these sections, not only because they relate to subjects of practical instruction, but because they give a practical exposition of ideas which, as appears from the evidence put before us, are largely unfamiliar in the National Schools of Ireland. But there are other features of the Kindergarten the extension of which we regard as equally [illegible] elements of a complete education for the older children. We refer to the large part played in the Kindergarten by singing, and by rhythmical movement of various kinds. We cannot regard the curriculum of any school as satisfactory which does not make reasonable provision for appropriate physical exercises, and for progressive advancement in the knowledge and practice of vocal music. These subjects, the latter particularly, do at present receive attention in many of the primary schools of Ireland, and they are cultivated in some of these schools with marked success; but we would desire to see both one and the other, if possible, included in the curriculum in all cases. We also think it important that they should be taught, not perfunctorily, but with a due appreciation of the ends they are to serve in a well-balanced scheme of education.

There is one feature of Kindergarten teaching, which is of special importance in its application to the work of the higher classes. We refer to the manner in which the songs, the games, and the occupations of the Kindergarten from time to time centre round some common idea, and are made to illustrate and reinforce each other. We shall have occasion to indicate in succeeding sections of our Report how this principle applies in the case of several subjects with which we deal specially; how, for example, drawing and manual exercises are intimately related to each other, and how their effectiveness as instruments of education can be greatly enhanced when this connection is kept in view. We shall also point out how instruction in elementary science, if properly given, may be made to bear upon other branches of schoolwork, and contribute to their efficiency. *Part II. Section I. Kindergarten.*

But we wish specially here to insist upon the importance of this principle of the interpenetration of school subjects in the case of the "three R's." We believe that the instruction in these subjects can be made more vivid and more effective when the pupil is made to realise that they are not merely abstract studies, but have a direct applicability to other subjects, and to the real needs of life.

Arithmetic, for example, acquires a new interest for the children when it is applied to the solution of some problem that arises in the course of other studies, or when it is linked in some way with their every day experience. Reading is more valued when it is found to be a key to information on matters as to which their curiosity has already been aroused by other lessons. Composition is more interesting and gives a better mental training when it consists, not in writing essays on abstract subjects, about which the children have really nothing of their own to say, but in the careful statement of facts of their own observation and experience.

We conclude, therefore, that if, in pursuance of the ideal of complete education revealed in the Kindergarten, subjects of practical instruction such as those referred to above receive, as we recommend they should, greater prominence in the school curriculum, progress in the "three R's" need not be appreciably less, and the work done in them may have a greater intellectual and practical value. They may become in themselves subjects of Practical Instruction.

But to attain this end, it is essential that the Kindergarten ideal should be kept steadily in view at all stages of education. The various subjects of practical instruction must be regarded as integral parts of the school work, and not merely as subsidiary subjects, to be taken in such fragments of time as can be spared from instruction in the "three R's." These in themselves should be regarded only as instruments of education.

Ability to pass mechanically the words in a reading book is of little value as an end in itself. It is only a means to an end, and the duty of the school is not completely discharged until the child has been put in the way of applying its knowledge. Further, it is neither necessary nor desirable that the mechanical power of reading should come first, and its practical application after. Rather, the two objects should be associated from an early stage. In the same way, writing and arithmetic should not be treated in the school as ends in themselves, but largely as valuable instruments for rendering knowledge clearer and more exact, and the practical application of them should be kept in view from a very early stage.

It appears to us to be a fair inference from the evidence that exclusive or almost exclusive devotion to the "three R's" tends to defeat its own ends, and we consider that even in these subjects better results might be obtained if a broader conception of the true aim of education prevailed. We consider that the method of inspection at present in force in Ireland and the mode of assessing the value of the work done in the subjects tend to obscure this broader conception of education, and to give undue prominence to merely subordinate aims; and accordingly in the third part of our Report we suggest some modifications of the system, which, if carried out, would, perhaps, do something to redress the balance.

II.—EDUCATIONAL HANDWORK.

Except in the case, already mentioned, of the Kindergarten Occupations in the Infants' Classes, it is only within comparatively recent years that Handwork—whether of an elementary character, such as paper-folding and cardboard work, or of a more advanced character, such as woodwork—has been introduced, with the sanction of any public educational authority, as a part of the work of primary schools in the United Kingdom. But the view that such manual exercises should have a place in the curriculum of a primary school is far from being a new one. Even in the seventeenth and eighteenth centuries this view was warmly advocated by not a few of the leading educational reformers of the time, including Pestalozzi. *Section II. Educational Handwork. Handwork in primary schools.*

The main ground, and in most cases the only one, relied upon by many of those who first advocated the introduction of manual exercises into the schools, was that the training given by such exercises tended to equip children of the artisan and labouring classes with that manual skill which in after-life would be of value to them in the occupations by which they were to earn their bread.

Part II, Section II. [illegible]

But even from the beginning it was seen by some educational reformers, and it is now being recognised more and more, that such exercises have a claim to a place in the curriculum of the primary school, quite independent of that on which their introduction might be advocated in the special interests of those children who are to earn their livelihood by manual work.

In the first place it is felt that even primary education has a scope wider than the teaching of reading, writing, and arithmetic, or even than the development of the intellectual faculties in general, and that some cultivation of manual dexterity for its own sake may fairly claim to be a proper object of every well-ordered system of primary education. It is maintained too by writers of authority that the cultivation of manual dexterity reacts advantageously upon the intellectual faculties, and is an important aid to their development. Recent physiological research gives support to this contention. It is stated by high authorities in this department of research that the development of what are known as the higher brain centres is intimately connected with the development of the motor centres which control the action of the hand, and which in their turn depend for their development on the exercise of that organ. In any case it is a matter of experience that manual exercises of the kind to be described in this section of our Report do, in fact, constitute an instrument in some respects more suitable and convenient than other school studies for attaining certain intellectual and moral results which are of high value in the training of the child.

Educational aspect of Manual Training.

What these results are, and in what manner they are to be attained, will be more conveniently described in connexion with the particular exercises dealt with in the sequel.[1] But we may here, for the sake of clearness, distinguish, in accordance with the view now generally accepted, between two objects aimed at in the practice of manual exercises in school,—the direct and the indirect. The direct object is the acquirement by the children of a general manual dexterity, which shall render the hand a more efficient servant of the brain in all circumstances. It is to be observed that even from this point of view, it is a general manual dexterity that is to be aimed at, not the special dexterity suitable to a particular trade. The indirect object is the mental and moral discipline referred to above. Of the two objects, although the first is not to be neglected, and although it cannot be neglected if the second is to be attained, the second is, for school purposes, incomparably the more important, and must be the main consideration in determining the course of instruction to be pursued. Experience shows that it is this aspect of school manual exercises which teachers are most likely to overlook, and it therefore requires to be dwelt upon with greater insistence. We shall have frequent occasion to refer to it in the following pages. For convenience we shall designate it the educational aspect of manual training.

History of the movement.

In the early history of the Manual Training movement, however, the distinction which we have just pointed out was only fitfully recognised, and even the direct object of school manual exercises was not always correctly apprehended. The only view that was then at all generally acted upon, was that such exercises provided a form of training useful to children of the artisan and labouring classes.

The German "Schools of Industry."

In accordance with this idea, schools known as Schools of Industry were established during the last century in many parts of Germany. These were established as primary schools; but—as is lucidly pointed out in an instructive Memorandum kindly prepared for the use of this Commission by Mr. M. E. Sadler, of the English Education Department[2]—the system which these schools embodied was quite at variance with sound principles of primary education, and it is not to be wondered at that they failed. Two causes have been assigned for their failure. First, it has been pointed out that, in the excess of their zeal for training in manual work as such, they altogether neglected to turn this training to account for the attainment of any object of a general educational character. Again, the training in manual work given in the German Schools of Industry is said to have been a form of technical instruction, adapted to the requirements of particular trades, and therefore quite out of place in a primary school, where such specialised instruction was given prematurely, and to the disadvantage both of primary education and of technical secondary education.

Pestalozzi.

It was on the score of the industrial or economic advantages of manual exercises, rather than in view of their advantages for the purposes of general primary education,

[1] See especially pp. 16–21, 23, 73, 80.

[2] Appendix A, V. Memorandum on Manual Training for Boys in Primary Schools in Foreign Countries; by M. E. Sadler, Director of Special Inquiries and Reports to the Committee of Council on Education.

that Pestalozzi at first advocated the introduction of this branch of school-work. In his later writings, however, he modified his earlier view, and laid stress on the general educational purposes that could be served by the special training given by manual exercises in the school. But his change of view came too late. We quote from Mr. Sadler's Memorandum:— Part II. Section II. Historical Summary. Mr. Sadler's Memorandum.

> "This side of Pestalozzi's teaching received comparatively little attention, at least so far as the curriculum of the elementary school was concerned. . . . In the sphere of primary education, manual training had become identified with the philanthropic industrial [illegible] exemplified by the Schools of Industry. Pestalozzi's followers therefore did not grasp [illegible] their master's view that manual training and other forms of teaching should be combined together.
>
> "The result was that the primary school, though owing the greater part of its improvement to the influence of Pestalozzi and his followers, gradually became too literary in its curriculum, and the last thirty years have seen unavailing efforts to remedy defects which would never have become serious had Pestalozzi's doctrine been adopted and applied in its entirety."

The last thirty or forty years may be taken as the period within which the movement now in progress for the introduction into primary schools of a system of manual exercises arranged with a view to their general educational advantages, had its beginning. It is convenient to follow in outline Mr. Sadler's instructive Memorandum in tracing the present position of this movement in various countries. The Memorandum deals only with countries outside the United Kingdom.

FINLAND.—Within the present century, Finland was the first country to give a recognised place in the curriculum of the primary school to woodwork and other manual exercises. That it did so was in great measure due to the influence of Uno Cygnaeus (1810-1888). His project for the re-organisation of the primary schools of that country was carried into effect during the years 1858-1866. Cygnaeus laid great stress on the general educational discipline given by manual exercises, as distinct from the economic advantage to be derived from the early acquisition of manual skill. In 1866, instruction in some branch of manual work, such as woodwork, basket work, [illegible] work, or iron work, was made compulsory in the Training Colleges for male teachers, and in all primary schools for boys in country districts. Finland.

NORWAY.—In Norway this branch of school-work was first recognised in the official programme in 1860. It is only within recent years that much attention has been given to the usefulness of a system of manual exercises as a branch of general primary education. Since 1891 it has been compulsory in all Norwegian Training Colleges and town schools. Norway.

SWEDEN.—In Sweden the movement for manual work in the schools was at first an effort to revive the old Swedish tradition of domestic industry. Fortunately the experience of Finland led the Swedish authorities to encourage the strictly educational side of the work, and to connect it, under the name of Sloyd, with the elementary school curriculum. Sweden.

In 1875, the well-known training school for teachers of Sloyd, at Nääs, not far from Gothenburg, was established by a local landowner, Herr Abrahamson. The work of this training school, which for years has been under the direction of Herr Abrahamson's nephew, Herr Otto Salomon, has been one of the most important agencies in disseminating throughout Northern Europe a knowledge of the theory and practice of woodwork as a branch of the work of the primary school. It is stated that 2,400 teachers of Sloyd (including 800 foreigners) had been trained at Nääs down to 1895.

In 1896, instruction in Sloyd woodwork was given in 2,000 schools in Sweden, and in all the seven Training Colleges of that country.

DENMARK.—For some years after the introduction of manual work in the Danish schools, the industrial or economic view of the subject prevailed. The results are said to have not been satisfactory. In 1883, greater prominence was given to the educational idea. But this branch of school-work does not appear as yet to have made much progress in Denmark. Denmark.

HOLLAND.—Under the Code of 1889, manual school-work is a compulsory subject in the Training Colleges for men. There are also courses to enable adult teachers to acquire skill in giving instruction in manual work. Holland.

BELGIUM.—Instruction in manual work, such as woodwork, is given in many of the Belgian Training Colleges, but the subject is not obligatory either in the Training Colleges or in the schools. In many districts, however, advantage has been taken of the law of 1884, which empowered local authorities to introduce manual work as a school subject. Belgium.

AUSTRIA.—Since 1883 this subject has been recognised as an optional branch of school-work in Austrian town schools. Of late years, special attention is being given to it in Vienna. Austria.

C

Part II. Section II. Foreign Countries.

Hungary.

HUNGARY.—In Hungary, about twenty years ago, a strong movement was started in favour of manual work in elementary schools. But the object in view was the encouragement of domestic industries, and the movement ended in failure. Of late, an effort is being made to revive the movement, the educational idea now receiving prominence.

Germany.

GERMANY.—In Germany, the false start originally made by the establishment of the Schools of Industry naturally put a serious obstacle in the way of the introduction of woodwork and other manual exercises as a part of primary education. But now, throughout Germany, there is in progress a movement for this purpose, thoroughly inspired by the educational idea, and this movement is steadily gaining ground.

Until very recently, the movement in Germany had to depend exclusively on private effort. Its chief support came from an energetic Association, the German Association for Manual Work for Boys. A great number of the best teachers of this branch of school-work in Germany have been trained in a Training College established by this Association at Leipzig, under the directorship of Dr. Götze, who is one of the leaders of the movement throughout Germany. This College is open to foreign students, and has been largely attended by them.

The movement in Germany has at length won its way so far as to have its claim recognised for State-aid to the work it has undertaken to promote. The Governments of Prussia, Saxony, and Baden, now make State contributions in aid of this branch of school-work.

Manual exercises of various kinds have been introduced, as yet, into only 400 schools in Germany; many of these are private schools. Woodwork is taught in 300 schools; metal-work in 83; cardboard work in 223. In many of the German Training Colleges provision is now made for training the teachers to give instruction in these and similar subjects.

Switzerland.

SWITZERLAND.—In Switzerland the movement began in 1882. Already it has made considerable progress. Of the twenty-five Swiss Cantons, nineteen have made provision for woodwork and other manual exercises in the schools. The expenses are borne to a large extent by public funds. The Federal Government bears the whole cost incurred by the Training Colleges in the special training of teachers for this department of school-work.

Except in one or two Cantons, woodwork is not an obligatory subject in the schools of Switzerland. In some Cantons, however, it is obligatory in the Training Colleges. Courses of instruction in it are given at various centres by the Swiss Manual Training Union, and these are attended each year by about a hundred teachers.

France.

FRANCE.—In 1882 a law was passed making manual work such as woodwork, involving the use of the principal tools, obligatory in the elementary schools of France. It would seem, however, that this was done without the requisite preliminary steps being taken. Although the enactment was a compulsory law, nothing seems to have been done for the special training of the teachers: it is sufficiently obvious that in the absence of very ample provision for such training, the carrying out of such an enactment was a matter of absolute impossibility. Besides, there was another fatal element of weakness. At the outset, no doubt, great prominence was given in those official declarations that manual exercises were to be introduced into the schools in view solely of the importance of such exercises for the purposes of general education, and not as a mere preparation for manual work in after-life. But this view was frequently overlooked in the actual working of the system, in so far as the system came into operation at all. In practice, it was worked mainly with the view of preparing school-boys for the manual occupations by which they were to earn their bread. Now, however, the educational idea is beginning to get prominence. In Paris, a programme admirably arranged on educational lines is in operation in the city schools. Throughout the country as a whole, the law of 1882 would seem to a large extent to have remained a dead letter.

United States.

UNITED STATES OF AMERICA.—In the United States the development of school instruction in woodwork and other kinds of manual work has been very rapid during recent years. This is so especially in the States of New York and Massachusetts. The idea of the general educational value of such instruction, as distinct from its merely economic or industrial utility, seems to be kept well in view.

General results.

It is clear from the information thus given in Mr. Sadler's Memorandum, that, outside the United Kingdom, only moderate progress has as yet been made in any country, with

Part II. Section II. European Experience.

the exception of Finland, Norway, and Sweden, towards the introduction of manual exercises in any systematic form as a part of the general educational work of the State-aided primary schools.

Reports of Assistants.

The information we have obtained through the Reports[1] of the Assistants whom we were enabled to send to visit schools in Belgium, France, Germany, Holland, and Switzerland, leads substantially to the same conclusion.

These Reports, however, are specially instructive. For, in addition to the valuable information contained in them in reference to many incidental points of great practical utility, they make two things abundantly clear. First, they show that in each of these countries there is a number of earnest workers, profoundly impressed with a sense of the high educational value of a well-organised system of manual training in a primary school. Again, we learn from them that in each country, the leaders of the movement are sustained by sufficient support from amongst the public to have secured practical recognition for this branch of school-work in some towns or districts of each country. It would seem that the mistakes which were made in the earlier experiments are being corrected, and that progress is being made, however slowly, in proportion as mistaken opinions are removed, and clearer views obtained of the true function of manual exercises in a scheme of elementary education.

Division of subject.

It will, we think, be convenient to place under distinct headings the further observations which we have to make upon the subject of Educational Handwork. Under the first heading, "Hand and Eye Training," we shall deal with exercises of a simpler character, such as paper-folding and the like. Under the second heading, "Woodwork: Sloyd," we shall deal with exercises of a more advanced character.

Hand and Eye Training.

A development of the Kindergarten.

A very few years' experience of the working of the new methods introduced into the Infants School from the Kindergarten system were sufficient to show that, through the special training which they give to the eye and to the hand, the Kindergarten Gifts and Occupations serve an educational purpose of great utility. It came then to be recognised as desirable that the range of usefulness of this new branch of school-work should be extended, by the introduction of similar training, in some more advanced form, into the higher classes of the school.[2]

England.

In England, the introduction of Educational Handwork of any kind in classes outside the Kindergarten department, was first authorised by the State in 1890, when Woodwork was recognised as a school subject in the Standards above Standard IV.[3]

Soon afterwards, it came to be felt that there was a gap between the Infants Classes and the Standards V. and VI., and courses comprising various graded manual exercises suited to the capacities of the children were devised to fill this gap.[4] To the courses thus introduced we find it convenient to apply the term "Hand and Eye Training." We have found this term so used in several places in England, especially at Birmingham;[5] and, although it does not fully indicate the educational purpose and results of the exercises in question, nor indicate in any way their intermediate character, between the Kindergarten Occupations in the Infants Classes, and the Woodwork and similar manual work in the upper Standards, we adopt it as a convenient expression, already in recognised use in the sense in which we propose to use it.

The term "Hand and Eye Training."

The objects aimed at.

In the Irish National Schools, the use made of the Gifts and of the Occupations of the Kindergarten system in the Infants Classes is not followed up by any organised course of Hand and Eye Training in the other classes of the school. The subject being thus, in fact, in Ireland, so far as concerned, a practically unknown one, we consider it essential to state distinctly the objects to be aimed at in any course of Hand and Eye Training in primary schools, and the lines on which this special branch of school-work should be carried out: we shall do this, as far as possible, in the words of a number of witnesses whose evidence we have received, and who are eminently entitled to be considered experts in relation to it. For the same reason we think it necessary also to describe in somewhat full detail the nature or scope of the exercises by which this training is given in schools which we visited in England.

---

[1] Appendix B, Reports of Assistants.
[2] Evid., Vol. ii., [illegible], 9913.
[3] Ibid., [illegible], 9914-6.
[4] Ibid., [illegible], 9954-5, 9986-7, [illegible]; [illegible], 10031-10038.
[5] Ibid., [illegible], 9163-7.

Part II. Section II. Experimental Exercises. Hand and Eye Training.

The object of all such exercises is to train the eye to accuracy and rapidity in observation, the hand to skill in execution, and the mind to a sense of the importance of truthfulness in work. These exercises also teach the children not only to observe, but to interpret what they observe, and to describe it. They cultivate habits of neatness, of orderly arrangement, of accuracy in measurement, of attention to small and apparently trifling details—habits which cannot fail to be of use to the children in after-life, no matter what may be the trades, professions, or occupations in which they may be engaged, or the positions which they may have to fill. The courses of Hand and Eye Training have the further advantage of providing a series of educational exercises especially useful for children of the class described to us by many witnesses as the less "bookish" class: to such children these exercises give a chance of excelling, by giving them something to do which they may be able to do well. Experience has shown that the new occupation thus given has, in addition to its many direct advantages, the effect of arousing dull children to an earnest, and often successful, effort to overcome the difficulties that retard their progress in the other branches of school-work.[1]

Materials.

For the exercises in Hand and Eye Training, various materials have been utilised; the principal being paper, plain and coloured; cardboard; wire; and modelling-clay.

Courses.

In England, where special attention has been directed to the organisation and development of this branch of school-work, the courses followed in different districts, and sometimes even in different schools within the same district, differ widely from one another, that is, they differ in the special exercises by means of which the training is given; but all the courses that we have seen in operation are controlled by the same general principles. In all cases of successful teaching, the results we have above enumerated are obtained. In some cases, however, the importance of accuracy is emphasised; in others, attention is given more particularly to the cultivation of the reasoning powers; in others, again, the special aim of the exercises is the development of originality, or of artistic feeling. In most cases drawing is treated as an integral part of the work.

Birmingham.

As an example of the exercises by which the educational objects of a course of Hand and Eye Training are sought to be attained, we shall take the exercises in paper-folding which we saw in operation in Standard I., in a school that we visited at Birmingham.

Paper-folding.

In paper-folding, the object first aimed at is to bring the children to appreciate form. A child has to compare the size and form of a piece of paper held in his hand with the size and form of a representation of the same piece of paper, drawn by the teacher upon the blackboard. Different forms also are to be compared and contrasted. For this purpose, squares, oblongs, and diamonds are obtained by folding different pieces of paper, and the corresponding figures are drawn by the teacher on the blackboard. Then the child is led to compare the figures, to observe the difference between them, and to express that difference in his own words, as best it can.

Next comes another form of paper-folding exercise. Each child holds a piece of paper, all the pieces being identical in form and in size. A representation of the paper is drawn by the teacher on the blackboard, and after each child has got the paper into the position represented by the drawing, the teacher indicates on the blackboard, by an alteration in the drawing, that a certain portion of the piece of paper held by the child is to be folded over, backwards or forwards as the case may be. The children are thus trained both to interpret drawings, and to carry out the directions which the drawings convey. After they have made the first fold, so as to bring the form of the paper into accordance with that represented by the altered drawing on the blackboard, alteration after alteration is made in the drawing, each of which indicates some new fold that is to be made. As each successive direction is thus given, the children fold the paper in the way indicated. In the end, frequently to their surprise and delight, the paper is found to have assumed the shape of some familiar object.

Educational advantages.

The educational advantages[2] of such exercises are obvious. The powers of observation of the children are exercised and strengthened by the attention which they must give to each direction given by the teacher through the successive changes in the drawing on the blackboard. The reasoning powers are cultivated in the mental effort which has to be made in carrying out the direction given by the drawing, so as to

---

[1] Ibid., vol. II., [illegible], [illegible]; [illegible], 3423, [illegible]; [illegible], 1874; [illegible], [illegible]; [illegible], [illegible]; [illegible], [illegible]; [illegible], [illegible].

[2] Ibid., vol. II., [illegible], 3487; [illegible], [illegible]; [illegible], [illegible]; [illegible], [illegible]; [illegible], [illegible]; [illegible], [illegible]; [illegible], [illegible]; [illegible], [illegible]; [illegible], [illegible].

bring the paper into the very shape indicated. Habits of accuracy are formed by the exactness with which each fold, even the simplest, must be made. A sense also of the importance of carefulness in work is engendered by the necessity of watchfulness in comparing the folded paper, after each step in the process, with the drawings on the blackboard. The interest of the children, as we had more than one opportunity of observing, is well sustained by their rivalry in working out the exercises, and also, to some extent, by the nature of the objects represented by the paper when the folding has been completed.

It will be observed from the nature of this exercise that the lesson which it gives the children in the importance of carefulness and of accuracy is a very practical one; for if at any stage of the process a slip be made, either in the reading of an indication given on the blackboard, or in the making of a fold, the child will very soon discover that the mistake, trifling as it may seem in itself, has made the completion of the exercise impossible.

Gradation of Exercises.

Exercises in paper-folding can, of course, be given of every required degree of difficulty, from the very simplest up to the most complex. The educational usefulness of the exercises, and even the possibility of having them worked by the children at all, must largely depend upon the judgment of the teacher in selecting for the children, at each stage in their progress, exercises that will neither be too easy nor too difficult for them. A manual of directions is, no doubt, provided for the guidance of teachers; but no fixed rules can of themselves always secure the selection of the particular exercises most suitable for a class, in view of the capacity of the children and of the progress which they have already made. Good judgment on the part of the teacher is, perhaps, still more important as to the amount of guidance to be given to the children in keeping them clear of the danger of mistakes at critical points, and as to the opportunities, or even the help, that may be given to them for the discovery and timely correction of mistakes.

In each successive Standard some new material is introduced for the working of the exercises. It would be out of place here to go through them in detail; we may, however, briefly mention that in the carefully-planned system of Hand and Eye Training in use at Birmingham, the exercises in Standard I. deal only with plane surfaces: paper-folding is probably the best example of exercises of this class. In Standard II. the idea of a solid is introduced by means of interesting exercises worked out with small blocks of wood in the shape of cubes and other rectangular figures. Each child in the class is provided with a small box of these, and the exercises consist in the placing of these successively in position, as directed by the teacher. In these exercises also, the directions are given by the teacher drawing upon the blackboard. A representation, in succession, of each little block as it is to be placed, is drawn by him in plan and in elevation: in the end, when each block has been placed in the position shown by the drawing, some structure, interesting in design, which the teacher had in view throughout, is found to have been formed. It will be seen that the general idea underlying these exercises is the same as that underlying the paper-folding exercises of Standard I., and that they form a simple but practical introduction to a method of representing solid forms on paper.

The course for Standard III. comprises also some interesting exercises in the making of knots and the tying of little parcels. In these exercises also, the work to be done at each step is indicated by drawings made by the teacher on the blackboard.

In the knot-tying exercises we were much struck by the ease with which a number of the children were able to interpret even those drawings that represented some particularly complicated series of interlacings. Several of the children were able from a mere inspection of the drawing, at once to state what the result would be if the ends of a string, loosely interwoven in the manner represented on the blackboard, were pulled in opposite directions,—whether any knot would be formed, and if so, what kind of knot it would be.

The Birmingham course of Hand and Eye Training has sometimes been criticised on the ground that it makes too great a demand upon the mental capacity of the children.[1] But in so far as this criticism may be to any extent well founded, it would only go to show that the unquestionably sound principles upon which this admirable system has been constructed by Mr. Bevis, the Director of Manual Training under the Birmingham School Board, have not, in all cases, been judiciously applied. It would seem to us, however, that the criticism must be taken as applicable to the occasional selection of some unduly difficult exercise by an injudicious teacher, rather than to any defect in the system itself.

[1] Ibid., vol. ii., [illegible].

Part II. Section II. Hand and Eye Training. London. Coloured work.

In the Hand and Eye Training Course of the London School Board, coloured work holds a prominent place. Special importance is attached to it by Mr. Vaughan, the Organising Teacher of Hand and Eye Training under that Board.[1]

We may here mention that one of the points to which Mr. Vaughan directed our attention was the interesting one that, in the very early stages of children's drawing, an important advantage is secured by their having a coloured pattern to copy from, even though they are not themselves to copy it in colours. For when the figure before them is a coloured one, they are less likely than they otherwise would be, to look merely to the separate lines of which the figure is formed. The colour directs their attention to the figure as a whole; and when various parts of it are differently coloured, their attention is thus directed to the relative size of each of those parts, in relation to the other parts and to the whole. Thus, by the introduction of coloured work in the earliest stages of the Hand and Eye Training course, not merely are the children led to take an intelligent interest in contrasts and harmony of colour, and even to form for themselves little patterns and designs, but, indirectly, an important step is taken towards the correction of that most common defect in children's rudimentary attempts in drawing—the want of attention to proportion.

Results obtained.

As to the results of the introduction of the Hand and Eye Training courses, we have received much valuable information.

We recognise that where there is a well-balanced school curriculum for general education, it is difficult to ascribe any special feature of mental or moral development to any special section of the work of the school. But many of those whose evidence we have taken in reference to the Hand and Eye Training exercises were in a position to speak of the results of the introduction of those exercises from personal knowledge of the schools both before they were introduced and afterwards. We cannot but regard it as a strong proof of the usefulness of this branch of school-work, that the testimony of those who have thus had an excellent opportunity of practically estimating its usefulness, is altogether to the effect that not only have the Hand and Eye Training exercises been effective in attaining the objects already mentioned as specially aimed at in their introduction, but that they have contributed notably to the improvement of the work of the school all round. We do not, in this, refer so much to the evidence, valuable as it is, which was given to us by teachers of the Hand and Eye Training courses. They perhaps might be supposed to take, not unnaturally, an unduly favourable view of the beneficial results of their own special work in the school. We refer rather to the strong concurrent testimony of others,—leading members of School Boards, Head Masters not themselves engaged in the teaching of these courses, Inspectors of Schools, and other leading authorities on educational subjects.[2]

Sir Joshua Fitch's testimony may be quoted as illustrating the general drift of the evidence to which we thus refer. "I think," he said, "that all teachers who have adopted these methods have found that they quicken the general intelligence of the scholars, and at the same time give to many scholars who are not bookish a chance of attaining excellence, and of doing something which they can do well. It has a very good influence upon their general training." And, after deprecating the exaggerations of enthusiasts who are "disposed to think that the world is going to be regenerated by turning schools into workshops," he added that "within the proper limits, the carrying forward of some form of manual instruction right through the whole scheme of education, up to the secondary school, is a step in the right direction, and has done distinct good."[3]

By Head Masters of schools, not themselves specially engaged in the teaching of the Hand and Eye Training courses, we were informed in detail of many beneficial results of this training:—It makes the children alert; it makes them more intelligent; it is entirely a training of the intelligence, and there is no getting off with guesswork; it cultivates the power of rapid observation; it makes the children, from the very first, attach great importance to exactness; it goes to develop the inventive faculty; it is a relief to the children, by varying the nature of their school work; refreshed and brightened by it they have greater zest for their book-work; it has been found an effectual check to truancy; it gives a dull child the chance of getting on to the same plane with smarter children, and thus gives to dull children a useful incentive to

---

[1] Evid., vol. ii., Vaughan, [illegible]; see also Appendix A, XXX.

[2] Evid., vol. ii., [illegible]; Evid., vol. iv., [illegible].

[3] Evid., vol. ii., [illegible].

exertion in the other work of the school; the exercises in it are the most popular with the pupils; it thus helps in keeping up the attendance in the school; it improves the teachers too, giving them increased tact and skill.[1]

Several witnesses bore testimony to the opportunity which the Hand and Eye Training exercises afford of supplementing the instruction in other branches of school-work. Thus, drawing is intimately connected with most forms of Hand and Eye Training, even in its elementary stages;[2] this is plain from the description already given of the exercises which we witnessed at Birmingham. The power of correct grammatical expression is given by causing children, during the exercises in Hand and Eye Training, to express themselves with correctness, and, at least within certain limits, to use complete sentences in answering questions, as well as in describing what they see or what they do.[3] In these exercises, arithmetic, too, may be incidentally illustrated and taught.[4] Clay-modelling, which in some courses of Hand and Eye Training, comes in at a very early stage, has been effectively turned to account for the illustration of geographical terms, and for the study of form.[5]

In reference to clay-modelling, in this aspect of it, we received some evidence of special interest from Mr. W. Marsh, the Head Master of a school at Barrow-in-Furness, in which clay-modelling by the children is made use of to bring home to them the meaning of geographical terms. Mr. Marsh finds that after half-a-dozen lessons in which the terms occurring in elementary geography are thus illustrated, the children, when asked what is meant by an island, an isthmus, a peninsula, and so on, can readily answer; and this is but natural, for, as he expressed it, "they are describing what they have really made, and not what we have told them."[6]

In connection with this application of an exercise in Hand and Eye Training to the teaching of geography, we do not think it out of place here to refer to an incident mentioned by the same Head Master in his evidence. It strikingly illustrates the elasticity of the system under which the work of the elementary schools is now tested by the Inspectors of the English Education Department, as contrasted with the rigid uniformity impressed upon the work of a school by the system of payment by results fees on the basis of an individual examination of the pupils, which still prevails in Ireland. When Her Majesty's Inspector first saw the clay-modelling in Standards I. and II. in Mr. Marsh's school, he was so satisfied that geography was excellently taught, that he would not further examine the subject.[7]

In view of the evidence we have received upon the subject, whether as regards the important objects which the exercises in Hand and Eye Training are designed to secure, or the satisfactory results that have been attained by the introduction of these exercises, we cannot hesitate to recommend that provision should at once be made for the introduction of courses of Hand and Eye Training in the Irish National Schools.

Such exercises obviously have a special utility in forming a natural link between the Kindergarten Occupations in the infants classes, and exercises such as those in Woodwork in the higher classes in the school. But we consider that their value is practically independent of this, and that they may be introduced with great advantage into schools where, from any cause, they may neither have been preceded by the Kindergarten Occupations on the one hand, nor be followed by more highly developed Manual Instruction, such as that in Woodwork, on the other.

Whilst we do not recommend that the Hand and Eye Training courses should, for the present, be made an obligatory part of the school programme, we consider that all possible encouragement should be given to the introduction of them, especially by the payment of a grant sufficient not only to remunerate the teacher, but also to cover the additional outlay entailed upon the school by the introduction of this new subject.

---

1 Evid., vol. II., [illegible]; [illegible]; Bass, 1666–71; [illegible]; [illegible].

2 Evid., vol. II., [illegible].

3 Evid., vol. II., [illegible].

4 Evid., vol. II., [illegible].

5 Evid., vol. II., Marsh, [illegible].

6 Evid., vol. II., [illegible].

7 Evid., vol. II., [illegible].

Part II. Section IX. Educational Handwork. Hand and Eye Training.

The evidence, however, shows that this cost is small, especially in the case of the earlier Standards or Classes.[1]

As regards the amount of time to be allowed to the exercises of the Hand and Eye Training course, the evidence also shows that 1½ or 2 hours per week is sufficient.[2]

Teachers.

It is necessary to add that we are impressed with the danger likely to result from such a branch of school work as this being taken up by incompetent teachers, especially by teachers who do not appreciate, or even comprehend, its educational aims. Experience in England has shown that teachers are sometimes led by the apparent simplicity of many of the exercises to think that the work is such as can be done by a teacher almost without any previous study or serious preparation of any kind. As a result, failing to comprehend the objects of the instruction, they content themselves with devising the shortest methods by which children can be drilled to perform the exercises with a certain mechanical accuracy, and thus they fail to secure the most useful results of this form of training.[3] We think it important, therefore, to insist that unless a teacher thoroughly grasps the object of these exercises, and has mastered the art of giving them intelligently to the children, the introduction of even the most skilfully devised course of Hand and Eye Training into a school is likely to do more harm than good.

While, therefore, we recommend that whenever a teacher shows both a desire and a capacity to take up a course of Hand and Eye Training for the children, every possible encouragement should be given to the experiment, and the most liberal allowance should be made for the inevitable shortcomings of all first efforts in an entirely new field of work, we consider it, on the other hand, essential that the Board of National Education should guard against this branch of school-work being undertaken by teachers who, though not really competent to take charge of it, might be tempted to do so by the prospect of earning the additional grants.

Objection to Results Fees System.

As regards the principle on which these grants should be assessed, we consider it obvious that in a branch of school-work such as this, the method of payment by results fees, on the basis of an examination of the pupils individually, is quite unsuitable.

In this, as in other branches of Manual and Practical Instruction, the point to be ascertained as a test of efficient work should not be the mere ability of the pupils individually to reproduce at an examination set exercises in which they have previously been drilled. The aim should rather be to test the intelligence and skill which the teacher brings to bear upon the work, and the extent to which the real purpose of the exercises as parts of a complete scheme of primary education is kept in view throughout. In particular, the Inspector should specially note whether the teacher is careful in excluding everything suggestive of the mere mechanical employment of the hands in the execution of set tasks, a process from which little, if any, educational advantage is to be gained.

The application of these remarks to various other branches of Manual and Practical Instruction, as well as to that with which we are here dealing, is obvious, and we do not think it necessary to repeat them in each instance. We shall, however, again refer to the matter in its general bearing, in the Third Part of our Report.

Grants for equipment.

It may be convenient here to make another remark which is of general application to the various branches of Manual and Practical Instruction.

The system on which grants are made to National Schools in Ireland is different from that followed in the case of the elementary schools of England and Scotland. In England and in Scotland, the grants are made to the managers of the schools, the managers being charged with the responsibility of maintaining the schools in a state of efficiency. In Ireland—except in the case of those Convent and Monastery Schools in which a Capitation payment takes the place of the payment of fixed salaries to the teachers according to their classification,—the grants made by the National Education Board are paid, not to the managers, but to the teachers.

The natural tendency of a system of payment such as that followed in Ireland is to check to some extent the introduction into the schools of any branch of instruction involving outlay for the providing of appliances of any kind. We do not suggest that

---

[1] [illegible], vol. II., [illegible], [illegible]; (see also Appendix A, XVII.); [illegible]; [illegible]; [illegible].

[2] [illegible], vol. II., [illegible]; [illegible]; [illegible]; [illegible].

[3] [illegible], vol. II., [illegible]; [illegible].

the system should be changed. But we consider that if Hand and Eye Training and other subjects of Manual and Practical instruction are to be placed, as they should be, in a prominent position in the system of National Education in Ireland, their introduction into the schools should be facilitated by special grants to the managers sufficient to cover the cost of providing the requisite outfit. Part II. Section II. Recommendations. Hand and Eye Training.

We would point out that a precedent for such grants already exists. When a new National School is opened, or an existing school is taken into connexion by the National Education Board, the Board makes a free grant of school requisites, such as school-books, maps, and the like.[1] It would not be an undue extension of the principle embodied in this arrangement, to apply it to the case of the introduction into a school of a branch of instruction which had not previously had a place in the educational system of the Board.

The arrangement in detail of the programme for the courses in Hand and Eye Training for the Irish National Schools will naturally devolve upon the National Education Board. In this important work, ample guidance, not only as to the general principles to be adhered to, but also as to all important details, will be found in the evidence received by this Commission.[2] The programme.

It will, we consider, be necessary for the Commissioners of National Education, especially in the beginning, to secure the services of some competent organisers, having experience in the practical work of Hand and Eye Training, to assist in the drawing up of detailed courses, and to superintend the introduction of them into the Irish National Schools. Organisers.

We would suggest that the official programme of the Board, whilst laying down in detail the lines of one or more well-considered courses of Hand and Eye Training, should make it clear that the courses thus set forth are intended only for the guidance of managers, and that any manager who may wish to introduce into his school a course of Hand and Eye Training upon any different line, will be afforded facilities for doing so.[3] We regard this branch of school-work as one in which it is especially desirable to encourage individuality in the teaching. The sanction, however, of the National Education Board should, of course, be obtained before any programme other than one officially recognised could be made the basis of work in any school. Variety in courses.

Woodwork: Metal.

The manual exercises of the Hand and Eye Training courses in the lower classes of the schools naturally lead up to similar exercises of a more advanced character in the higher classes. More advanced exercises.

But these exercises differ in value among themselves in difficulty, and in the nature of the training which they give. Some are very elementary; others admit of extensive development, and are suitable for advanced classes. In particular it seems to be agreed that exercises in cardboard admit of, or rather demand, a high degree of accuracy, and some amount of physical strength such as cannot be expected from very young pupils. These exercises are particularly suitable, as a rule, for children of Classes III. and IV., but they may be made sufficiently difficult and sufficiently varied to make them appropriate for even the highest classes. For this reason they may form a fairly effective substitute for Woodwork, but only in cases where considerations such as that of cost make the introduction of Woodwork impossible. Cardboard.

But there seems to be no question that for older children, that is, roughly speaking, for those from ten to fourteen years of age, wood has many advantages over every other material. Exercises in Woodwork admit of greater variety of manipulation, and of more exact gradation—a consideration of great importance. They make more demand on the intelligence, especially when associated with the making and the interpretation of drawings, and they have an obvious practical application which makes them more interesting to the children, who at this age become dissatisfied with what they consider purely occupations. Woodwork.

In London, Liverpool, and Birmingham, the advanced manual exercises in some of the schools which we visited are in Woodwork, in others they are in Metal-work. But Metal-work.

---

[1] "134 (a.) The Commissioners furnish gratuitously to each School a First Stock of suitable School Requisites, in proportion to the attendance of children." Rules and Regulations of the Commissioners of National Education in Ireland (June, 1896), page 39.

[2] See especially Evid., vol. ii., evidence of Ricks, [illegible], [illegible], [illegible], [illegible].

[3] Evid., vol. ii., Ricks, [illegible]; [illegible], [illegible]; [illegible], [illegible]; [illegible], [illegible].

Part II. Section II. Existing Manual Work: Metal-work.

the use of metal as a material for school exercises is comparatively rare, and as we do not consider that exercises in Metal-work can be regarded as at all generally applicable in Irish National Schools, we shall not further refer to the subject. If in any exceptional cases in Ireland such exercises are considered likely to be of practical advantage in a school, the evidence given before us by several witnesses in England will be found to contain much useful information in reference to them.[1]

"Handicraft" in the National Schools.

Woodwork, as a branch of instruction organised on sound educational lines, has as yet no place in the school programme of the Irish National Education Board.

Under the name Handicraft, a two years' course of manual exercises, mainly in woodwork, is provided for in the programme of the Board. This course, which was introduced in 1883, comprises instruction in a number of the ordinary operations of carpentry, with the addition of miscellaneous other matters such as the soldering of pieces of tin, the knocking out of broken panes of glass, and the making of paste and glue.[2] It does not appear to have been constructed with any very definite educational aim, and it seems to have been a failure from the beginning. In 1896, the Handicraft course was taught in only 13 National Schools in Ireland.

In the minds of teachers who have had no other conception of school Woodwork than that conveyed to them by the Handicraft Course, whether as set forth in the Board's programme, or as taught in some few schools, this course has created, not altogether unnaturally, a strong prejudice against the introduction of any course of Woodwork into the schools. All such work is contemptuously referred to as "wood chipping," and the "unscientific use of tools."[3] It is of the utmost importance that the teachers should be fully informed of the essential distinction between a course, such as the Handicraft Course of the existing programme, which is purely utilitarian in its aims, and a course of school Woodwork, constructed on sound educational lines, and made part of the work of the school in view solely of its general educational advantages. If this be not done, many of the teachers, failing to appreciate the distinction, will naturally regard as of little value any course of Woodwork introduced by the National Education Board in accordance with the recommendations of this Report. We fully concur in the view expressed by Herr Salomon to those members of our Commission who visited Sweden, that no one ought to be allowed to teach this or any other subject who does not believe in the value of the subject which he is to teach.[4]

Historical: National Education Board in 1837.

It is interesting here to note that, as far back as 1837, the importance of providing a course of instruction in manual work, comprising, doubtless, instruction in Woodwork, was recognised by the Commissioners of National Education in Ireland, and that the Commissioners, in their statement upon the subject, then took as their starting point a principle which is now accepted by all educational authorities as of fundamental importance in this matter. The Fourth Annual Report of the Commissioners, issued in 1837, contains the announcement that their Training College for teachers, then about to be established, was to include a department for scientific instruction, and that in this department were to be taught "in particular, those branches of science which have a practical application to husbandry and handicraft." The Report then continues as follows:—

"We also purpose having a school for industry in the immediate neighbourhood of Dublin, with workrooms . . . attached to it, and that those who attend it shall be practised at stated times in different descriptions of manual work. . . .

"Our object is not to teach trades, but to facilitate a perfect learning of them, by explaining the principles upon which they depend, and habituating young persons to expertness in the use of their hands."

It was further stated in the same Report that the manual training thus to be provided was to be obligatory on all teachers in training in the Normal School or Training College, and that similar instruction was to be given to the pupils in the Model Schools then intended to be established—these being schools which were to differ from the ordinary National Schools of the country in being under official management, so that the course of instruction to be given in them, even in the optional parts of the school programme, would be under the direct control of the Commissioners of National Education themselves.

---

[1] Evid., vol. ii., [illegible]; Riggs, [illegible]; Sunderland, [illegible]; Dalton, [illegible]; Ross, [illegible]; Cowman, [illegible].

[2] Rules and Regulations of the Commissioners of National Education in Ireland (June, 1896), pp. [illegible].

[3] Evid., vol. iii., Terence Clarke, [illegible]; Dughy, [illegible].

[4] Evid., vol. iv., Ward, [illegible].

[5] Evid., vol. iv., Salomon, [illegible].

Part II. Section II. Sloyd: School Handwork, Woodwork: Sloyd.

The distinction, so clearly apprehended by the Commissioners of National Education in 1837, between that form of manual training which, as it is of general educational value, is in place in a primary school, and the teaching of trades—a branch of instruction which should have no place in the work of such a school,—is a distinction of fundamental importance. It receives perhaps its clearest illustration in the matter with which we are dealing in this section of our Report.

This distinction is well pointed out by Herr Salomon, the director of the Training School at Nääs, in Sweden, for teachers of school Woodwork, or Sloyd, as it is termed in that country.

Educational woodwork. Herr Salomon.

"Sloyd," says Herr Salomon,[1] "is a system of educational handwork. On the continent, the term Sloyd embraces many useful forms of handiwork. The term Sloyd, in England, is generally understood to mean a system of handwork in wood. Why then do we not call it carpentry? Because it differs from carpentry in several essential features. . . . Carpentry is a trade, and the principles which underlie it are entirely utilitarian; whereas Sloyd is solely a means of formative education."

How it differs from carpentry.

As Herr Salomon goes on to explain, the purpose of this branch of school-work is quite different from that of instruction in the trade of carpentry. The object of Woodwork in the primary school is not to turn out carpenters, but to develop generally the faculties of the children. Nor is its usefulness in this respect confined to the development of their physical powers. It cultivates, no doubt, manual dexterity; but it also cultivates carefulness, self-reliance, accuracy, patience, perseverance, and other useful points of character. It trains too the faculty of attention, and develops the power of concentration. Indirectly, moreover, it has the advantage of inspiring a respect for the work of the artisan, and for those who are skilled in any branch of it.

This description of the aims and results of Sloyd, given almost in the words of Herr Salomon, has reference primarily to the Swedish system of school Woodwork. But it is equally applicable to the systems of Woodwork in use in the schools of other countries, in so far as those systems are constructed, as the Swedish system is, on truly educational lines. There is no reason therefore why the term Sloyd may not be applied to them.

The Swedish Sloyd System: The "Models."

This may be the most convenient place to state in outline the salient points of the Swedish system. That system is worked out through a series of objects, technically termed Models, which are to be made out of wood. These begin with some exceedingly simple objects, such as pointers, letter-openers, labels, and the like. In the typical Sloyd course for boys, at Nääs, there are fifty such Models, and thirty in the course for girls. They are so arranged that each represents some slight advance upon the one that preceded it in the course,—either some new tool, or some new use of a tool previously employed, being introduced in the making of it.

No division of labour.

The utmost importance is attached to having each object, when made, the work of one individual pupil. Division of labour is rigorously excluded from the system; so much so, that whenever it is necessary for the teacher to show the pupil how any particular part of the work is to be done, he is to show this, not by doing a portion of the pupil's work for him, but by giving the demonstration upon another piece of wood. Self-reliance is one of the points of character to be developed by the system, and so the Sloyd Model, when completed, must be, from beginning to end, the individual work of the pupil who made it.

Accuracy insisted on.

In the Swedish Sloyd system, mere approximations to accuracy receive no toleration. If, for instance, a piece of wood is cut to any appreciable degree too short for the particular Model that is to be worked out, it has to be put aside as unsuitable for the work then in hand. The same check upon inaccuracy is applied even in the case of an almost completed Model, if, after days of work, some want of attention to a minute detail has led to a mistake which makes it impossible to complete the work to the dimensions laid down in the drawing.

With the view of removing, as far as possible, all ground for misconception as to the nature and the objects of this branch of school-work—the subject being one that may very easily be misunderstood, especially in a country like Ireland, where, as yet, but very little is known about it either by teachers or by managers of schools,—we think it useful, also, to quote the following observations of Herr Salomon upon another point of considerable importance in the system.

The aim of Sloyd.

"The objects," says Herr Salomon, "which the child makes are equally useful with those of the carpenter; but, unlike the work of the carpenter, the value of the child's work does not exist in them, but in the child that made them.

[1] *The Theory of Educational Sloyd*, by Otto Salomon. London, 1892, page 3.

Part II. Section II. Educational Handwork. Woodwork: Slöjd.

"Many people object to this kind of instruction. 'It takes,' they say, 'ten hours to make a spoon [of wood]; why not buy one for 2d. or 3d.?' For exactly the same reason that we do not tell children to buy copybooks filled with writing, instead of filling them. It is not the filled copybook that we require in education; neither is it the spoon in Slöjd. Both are means having the same end in view—the development of the child. The destruction of the objects does not impair the faculties of the child, which were developed in making them, any more than the destruction of the copybook impairs the skilfulness of the child who filled it."[1]

This, in outline, is the Swedish Slöjd system. We have thought it useful to deal with it at some length, because, in our opinion, it admirably illustrates the fundamental principles upon which any system of Woodwork should be constructed, which is to form a part of the work of a primary school.

Woodwork in English and Scotch schools.

Both in England and in Scotland we found courses of Woodwork established as an important part of the work of many schools.

These courses follow in the main the principles laid down by Herr Salomon, though in some details they differ both from the Swedish system, and from one another. The differences regard chiefly the tools to be used, and the nature of the objects to be made. We do not consider that these differences are of sufficient importance to require any detailed consideration of them here. They are fully discussed in the evidence of various witnesses.[2]

Differences in details.

As an illustration of these differences in details we may, however, mention that in the Swedish system, the work to be done by the pupils, from the very first lesson, is the production of an object which, simple as it may be, is complete in itself. On the other hand, in the system most generally favoured in England, the pupil is at first taught merely the use of tools, through a series of exercises in planing, sawing, the making of joints, and the like.

In so far as both systems are worked out in England, the present tendency would seem to be for each to approximate to the other. We consider that when the programme in this subject is being arranged by the National Education Board, but little difficulty will be found in arranging a course combining the good points of both.

London.

In both England and Scotland, the introduction of Woodwork into the schools is of somewhat recent date. In London it was first introduced, merely as an experiment, and on a very small scale, by the London School Board in 1886. The experiment was considered successful, but as Woodwork was not then recognised by the English Education Department as a subject to be taught in Elementary Schools, the School Board was surcharged the amount expended. The work thus abruptly checked was not, however, abandoned. The Board was successful in obtaining through the City and Guilds' Institute a grant of £1,000 from the Drapers' Company, which enabled the experiment to be continued, and on a much larger scale, in the following year. This grant was administered by a Joint Committee, composed partly of members of the City and Guilds' Institute and partly of members of the London School Board, with subsequently some members of the Drapers' Company. So satisfactory were the results of the further experiment that the grant from the Drapers' Company was continued from year to year. A grant of £250 in aid of the work was also made from year to year by the London City and Guilds' Institute.

By means of the funds thus supplied, the Joint Committee was enabled to equip and maintain six Centres, in each of which instruction in Woodwork was given to the pupils of neighbouring Board and non-Board schools. In 1889, the Committee extended its sphere of work by establishing four Centres of instruction in laundry-work, which was not then recognised by the Education Department as a subject upon which the funds of a School Board could be expended.

In 1890, Woodwork (as well as laundry-work, which is dealt with in another section of our Report) was recognised by the Education Department as a school subject.

Part II. Section II. Educational Handwork: Woodwork, &c.

The School Board was thus enabled to expend its own funds upon this branch of school work. And in the same year money was provided by Parliament for grants for it from the Imperial Exchequer.

The Joint Committee still continues its useful work. It receives each year a grant of £1,000 from the Drapers' Institute and a grant of £250 from the London City and Guilds' Institute. Its chief aim for some years past has been to experiment in subjects of instruction not yet approved by the Education Department, and to provide instruction in Woodwork and other practical subjects, such as Metal-work for boys, and laundry-work and housewifery for girls, for the pupils of the non-Board schools which cannot afford the initial expense of starting such classes. It also maintains classes for the training of teachers in these various subjects.

The "Centre" system.

The "Centre" system,—that is, the system by means of which a room suitably equipped for instruction in Woodwork or in Metal-work is made available for the boys of several neighbouring schools,—is adopted also by the London School Board. There are now throughout London 180 such Centres, each affording space for either 20 or 40 boys. Room is thus provided for over [illegible] boys in all. But as each Centre is occupied by 10 relays of boys in the course of a week, the boys of each relay receiving instruction for two hours, the 180 Centres provide accommodation for the instruction of over [illegible] boys.

Under the rule of the London School Board, Woodwork or Metal-work, in so far as accommodation has as yet been provided for it, is an obligatory subject for boys above Standard IV. The Board's Report for 1896-7 shows that in that year the number of boys in the schools of the Board, receiving instruction either in Woodwork or in Metal-work, was [illegible].

Birmingham.

In Birmingham, the subject is, to the same extent, compulsory. The number of centres now provided is eight. Of these five are for Woodwork, and three for Metal-work. The number of boys in the Board's Schools attending the classes in Woodwork is 2,500, and the number attending those in Metal-work is 1,500, making a total of 4,000. Additional accommodation is now to be provided for 840 more boys in Woodwork, and for 660 in Metal-work, making, in all, 1,500, to meet the increasing demand.

Liverpool.

In Liverpool, under **similar arrangements, the number of boys attending the various** centres is [illegible].

Barrow-in-Furness.

In Barrow-in-Furness, where the arrangements **again are similar, the number** is [illegible].

Edinburgh.

In Edinburgh, Woodwork was first introduced six years ago, and then in only one school, as an experiment. It has now been introduced into 18 of the 31 schools under the Edinburgh School Board, and there is a general desire for the extension of it to all the schools. This is being done as expeditiously as possible. At present three additional schools are being provided with the requisite accommodation and outfit. It is not intended to adopt the Centre system. There is not, as yet, any rule of the Edinburgh School Board making Woodwork compulsory, but it is practically universal for boys of the Standards above IV. in all the schools where it has been introduced. The number of boys on the rolls of the Woodwork classes is [illegible].

Glasgow.

In Glasgow, as in the cities and towns which we visited in England, the instruction is given in Centres. Already Centres have been provided in which this instruction is given to the boys of [illegible] of the Glasgow Board Schools, out of a total of [illegible], and in consequence of the high opinion which has been formed of its educational value, it is being extended from year to year. As in Edinburgh, it is not compulsory. In Glasgow, up to the present, it is taken up mainly by boys of the Standards above the Fifth. The number of boys now attending the classes in the various centres is [illegible].[1]

Parliamentary Grant.

Both in England and in Scotland the Parliamentary Grant for Woodwork (and the same is true of Metal-work) in Elementary Schools was administered, up to March, 1899, not by the Education Department, but by the Science and Art Department, which has also had the administration in England and Scotland of the Parliamentary Grant for Drawing in the Elementary Schools. In both countries the Grant is henceforth to be administered by the respective Education Departments; but, so far as we have ascertained, no change has been made in the regulations under which grants for these subjects are made to the schools. These regulations are as follows:—

[1] See pages [illegible].
[2] See Appendix A., LXX.

Part II. Section II. [illegible]

The instruction must be in connection with Drawing, that is, the work of the pupils is to be done from drawings to scale previously made by them. The instruction, also, must be carried on continuously throughout the school year for two hours weekly, but the two hours may include one half hour for the special drawing in connection with the work. The work is to be done with the tools in ordinary use in handicrafts in wood or iron, and in a properly fitted workshop, wholly devoted to the purpose. The time given to this instruction must be in addition to the 20 hours per week prescribed as a minimum for the instruction in the compulsory subjects of the Codes of the Education Departments of England and Scotland.

The grants are made on the aggregate number of attendances made throughout the year by all the pupils who have made at least 10 attendances each. The payment is at the rate of 2d. per pupil for each attendance of two hours, with an addition of 20 per cent. if the instruction of the class be adjudged "excellent."

Progress.

Since the establishment of the system of Parliamentary grants for Woodwork, the number of schools in England and Scotland receiving grants for this subject has increased rapidly from year to year. This is shown by the following table[1]:—

Year ended 31st August.	Number of Schools.	Number of Pupils.	Amount of Grants.
			£
1891	[illegible]	[illegible]	500
1892	189	6,900	2,882
1893	362	17,851	4,397
1894	574	30,041	8,029
1895	905	47,485	14,234
1896	1,067	65,180	18,806

In 1897, there was a further increase. In that year the number of boys receiving this instruction was 106,348, and the amount of grants earned was £29,379, giving an average of nearly 5s. per pupil. Supposing one lesson to be given each week for forty weeks of the year, the maximum grant possible in respect of any pupil would be 6s. 8d., or (with the addition of 20 per cent.), 8s., in classes the instruction in which is reported "excellent."

Ireland.

These grants are paid only in respect of pupils in the Fifth or some higher Standard. They may be earned in all public Elementary Schools in which Drawing is taught, in England, Scotland, and Ireland, except schools under the Irish Board of National Education. Only two schools in Ireland receive the Grants of the Science and Art Department for Woodwork instruction[2]; both of these are under the care of the Christian Brothers. They are, the school of St. Vincent's Orphanage at Glasnevin, near Dublin, and the Christian Brothers' Day School at Limerick. In 1896, the former school received a grant of £[illegible] 6s. 7d., and the latter, a grant of £5 15s. 10d., making a total, for Ireland, of £[illegible] 2s. 5d.

The fee for "Handicraft."

In the Irish National Schools, the only grant at all corresponding to the grants of the Science and Art Department for Woodwork is a results fee of 5s. paid by the National Education Board in respect of pupils of the Fifth and Sixth Classes who pass the examination in the prescribed course in Handicraft.

The Report of the National Education Board for 1896 shows that, in that year, the number of pupils presented for examination in Handicraft, was 270, and that, of this number, 10 per cent. failed to pass. Even if all had passed, the

[1] Appendix to the Forty-fourth Report of the Science and Art Department, p. 379 (the figures for the two Schools in Ireland, which received grants for Woodwork, being deducted).

[2] Ibid., vol. [illegible], [illegible], 10503.

maximum grant payable would have been at the rate of 3s. per pupil. It is to be borne in mind that the grants of the Science and Art Department are paid in respect of the aggregate number of attendances, whilst the grant of the National Education Board, as it is a results fee, is payable only in respect of those pupils who pass the examination.

Part II. Section II. Kindergarten, Manual Instruction, Woodwork: Need of special grant.

In Ireland, there are no funds at the disposal of bodies, such as School Boards of many cities and towns in England and Scotland, nor resources of opulent societies, such as the London Guilds, available as aids either to the establishment or to the maintenance of this important branch of school-work. If, therefore, the pupils of the National Schools of Ireland are not to be excluded from the undoubted educational advantages which experience has shown to have resulted from the introduction of woodwork instruction in Elementary Schools in England and in Scotland, a special grant for the purpose of this instruction must be added to those now administered by the National Education Board.

The subject is one, the teaching of which involves not only a considerable initial outlay, but also a constant outlay from year to year. Before woodwork instruction can be introduced into a school, a room has to be built, or otherwise provided, for it; the room has to be fitted up with suitable benches; and a sufficient equipment both of tools and of material has to be supplied. The supply of material is a source of constant outlay. The tools, too, have to be kept in order, and they have also to be renewed from time to time.

Cost of equipment.

The evidence we have received from various witnesses shows that the initial cost of providing a Centre and equipping it, when a new building has to be erected for the purpose, is considerable. In Birmingham, such a Centre, fully equipped, was estimated to have cost about £480. Of this, £400 was estimated as the cost of the building, and £80, of the benches. The building is a detached one, and is of a permanent character, built of brick: it is meant for the instruction of 38 pupils at a time, and of 380 in the course of a week.[1] As was pointed out, however, by Mr. Sevin, the Director of Manual Training in the Birmingham School Board, a very suitable building could be provided at a cheaper rate. Still he considered that to provide a room which would accommodate 40 pupils at a time, and therefore 400 in the course of a week, £250 at least should be expended upon building alone.[1] His estimate of the annual cost of the work shows that this cost alone exceeds the amount of the grant received from the Science and Art Department.[2]

Our remarks as to cost have reference to the arrangements for woodwork instruction under the regulations of the Science and Art Department. These arrangements are comparatively costly, the conditions insisted upon being somewhat exacting. One result is that, in England and Scotland, Woodwork is practically confined to the schools of more or less important centres of population. In Sweden the case is different. As to this, we may quote from the special Memorandum drawn up for the information of our Commission by those members of it who visited that country. They inform us that, "on the whole, the lesson to be learned from Sweden in this respect is—with what modest and apparently incomplete provision of appliances the work can be carried on"; and, after giving several examples of the "makeshift arrangements" which are only now being generally replaced by separate fitted rooms, with a satisfactory equipment of benches, tools, and cupboards, they add that, "generally it may be said that in Sweden the question of material equipment is considered to be of altogether minor importance as compared with the finding of a teacher who is imbued with enthusiasm for the work, and who can conduct it with understanding and skill."[3]

Beneficial results.

The evidence we have received as to the beneficial results of the Woodwork instruction now given in the schools of England and Scotland is generally similar in character to that to which we have already referred in dealing with the Hand and Eye Training courses in the lower classes of the schools. We there quoted the emphatic testimony of Sir Joshua Fitch that "the carrying forward of some form of manual instruction right through the whole scheme of education up to the secondary school is a step in the right direction, and has done distinct good."[4] These words apply to the whole range of manual exercises, whether in their simpler forms, in the Hand and Eye Training courses, or in their more advanced forms such as Woodwork. But Sir Joshua Fitch's answer was given with special reference to those exercises in their more advanced form.

---

[1] Evid., vol. II., 3148-6. See also Evid., vol. II. [illegible], 4900-48; Sevin, 7283-8908.
[2] Evid., vol. II.: Sevin, 8870-78.
[3] Appendix to Third Volume of Evidence, p. 187.
[4] Evid., vol. II., 6647.

Part II. Section II. Evidence as to Manual Instruction. Woodwork & Sloyd.

The evidence of Sir Philip Magnus is equally noteworthy. He holds it to be "of the utmost importance that lessons in Woodwork should be a part of the ordinary curriculum of the school." In common with all the other witnesses who touched upon this aspect of the case, he points out that the object of those lessons should not be the teaching of a trade, but should be "the same as that of all the other instruction, the formation of character." "Of course," he says, "between the manipulation of wood by means of tools and the formation of character, there are naturally a great many steps. But instruction in woodwork may be made the means of training the hand and eye to accurate observation and skill in execution, to truthfulness in work, and to the acquisition of many of those habits which are of the utmost use to a child in after life . . . no matter what trade or occupation he may go to, whether he is likely to be a bricklayer, a watchmaker, a plumber, or engaged in any other trade . . . Or even if he went to an agricultural occupation, or into clerical work, the habits formed will be of the utmost use."[2]

It is unnecessary to multiply quotations in support of a **view as to which we found** absolutely no difference of opinion.

From witness after witness in England and in Scotland we learned, as the result of the experience gained since the establishment of the classes of Woodwork and similar instruction, that the instruction given in these classes is productive of the various advantages already specified in connection with the Hand and Eye training exercises in the lower standards. It trains and quickens the intelligence of the pupils. It teaches them, in many practical ways, the useful lesson of the importance of exactness even in matters of apparently small detail. It gives a useful variety to the work of the school. So far from injuriously affecting in any way the book-work of the school, it tends, on the contrary, to the greater progress of the pupils in that portion of their work. It is popular with the pupils, with their parents, and with the teachers. It has come to be popular even with teachers who at the outset were opposed to it, either from a misconception of its nature, viewing it as something connected with trades and therefore out of place in an elementary school, or from an apprehension, not unnatural in the absence of all experience as to its working, that it would interfere with the book-work of the school.[3]

We learned, moreover, that in addition to these numerous advantages, which are in some degree common to all manual exercises, whether of the simpler or of the more advanced form, Woodwork and similar instruction in the higher Standards has the further special advantage of giving an inducement to pupils, especially to those who have passed the standard of exemption from compulsory school attendance at an early age, to remain longer at school.[4]

Recommendation.

We recommend that a course of Woodwork, based on the lines of the Swedish system, with such modifications as the experience of other countries, especially of England and of Scotland, has shown to be useful, should at once be introduced into the programme of the National Education Board. It will obviously be necessary for the Board, in this case, as in the case of the Hand and Eye Training courses, to secure the services of competent organisers having practical experience in the work.

We do not consider that Woodwork should be made a compulsory subject. As to this, we direct attention to the evidence given by Herr Salomon. It is his opinion that one reason of the great and growing success of the Sloyd movement in Sweden is that in that country the subject has from the beginning been treated as an optional one. He gives some interesting figures. Sloyd was first introduced into the Swedish school programme in 1877. In the next year, the number of schools in which it was taught was 103. Nine years afterwards, in 1887, the number was 881. Seven years later, in 1894, it had grown to 1,887, or very nearly one-half of the total number of schools in Sweden.

In 1895, a different method of distributing the grant for Slöjd teaching was adopted, the new unit of distribution being, not a school, but a "division," each division being a class of from 10 to 15 pupils. In that year, grants were paid for 2,434 such classes. By way of contrast, Herr Salomon points to the case of France and Norway, where the mistake was made of introducing Woodwork as a compulsory subject. "The result," he says, "has been unsuccessful. If the subject be introduced on a small scale, it will grow; our experience in Sweden has shown that if we begin with small arrangements, they will grow more and more."[1]

So far from suggesting that the subject should be made compulsory in Ireland, we are strongly of opinion, for reasons similar to those stated by us in reference to the Hand and Eye Training course, that care should be taken by the National Education Board to hinder its being taken up by any but really competent teachers. Teachers.

Some of the evidence given to our Commission goes to show that in reference to this branch of school-work much has yet to be done for the education of the teachers themselves. We do not refer merely to the disadvantage at which the Irish teachers are necessarily placed from their never having received any training as teachers of this subject, and from their never having even seen anything of the actual working of it in the schools, which might in some measure have tended to qualify the older members of their body to give instruction in it. We refer rather to the lack of information shown, both as to the grounds on which the claim of such instruction to a place in a course of primary education is based, and as to the beneficial results which have followed from the introduction of it into the schools, wherever it has been introduced.

We also consider that the provision of a room giving sufficient accommodation for Woodwork instruction, and suitably equipped for the purpose, should be insisted upon. But we assume that, at least for some years in the beginning, the requirements of the National Education Board in this matter will not go beyond what is really essential, and we consider that in reference to it, the example of Sweden, to which we have already referred, rather than that of England or of Scotland, should be kept in view. Suitable equipment.

We have taken a good deal of evidence as to whether woodwork instruction in the schools ought to be given by teachers of the ordinary school subjects, specially trained for the purpose, or by artisan teachers.[2] The prevailing drift of the evidence is strongly in favour of the employment of ordinary school teachers. We fully concur in this view. We would refer specially to the evidence given on this point by Mr. D. Holland,[3] a teacher of considerable experience in a National school at Swords, near Dublin. Mr. Holland has himself endeavoured to do what can be done on the lines of the present Handicraft course of the National Education Board. Artisans or teachers.

A comprehensive statement of the reasons in favour of the employment of ordinary school teachers rather than artisans for the woodwork instruction will be found in Herr Salomon's treatise on the Theory of Educational Slöjd. These reasons presuppose that the artisan has not had the advantage of being trained as a teacher. Herr Salomon's fundamental reason is that woodwork exercises have a place in the elementary school just in so far as they serve purposes of general educational utility. In these exercises, neither the use of tools, nor the making of objects, is anything more than a means to an end. Dexterity of hand, though it is one of the results that may be attained, holds but a subordinate place amongst them. Slöjd is a means of education, and the teacher of it should be, first of all, not a mere workman, but an educator: the technical skill of the artisan may be greater than that of the teacher of ordinary subjects could be; but, from a Slöjd point of view, the amount of technical skill is of comparatively little importance. Moreover, in the case of an artisan instructor there is the positive drawback that it is, in most cases, much easier for him to do a thing himself, than to teach how it should be done, and so there is a danger of his giving the more help to the pupils than he should give, and a danger also of his giving it at

[1] Ibid., vol. iii., Salomon, 14931–4, 14947. See also Appendix to Third Volume of Evidence, p. [illegible].
[2] Ibid., vol. ii., [illegible]
[3] Ibid., vol. iii., Holland, 18123–39, 18155–6.

points where the pupils should rather be left to try to make out things for themselves, and to learn something for themselves, even from their own imperfect attempts and failures.

It is noted by Herr Salomon that, even as regards the Models themselves, the experience of Sweden goes to show that these are better turned out in schools where the instructor is a teacher of the ordinary subjects, than in those in which the instructor is an artisan. "All Swedish inspectors," he says, "who have reported on Slöjd say unanimously that the work produced by means of ordinary teachers is far superior to that produced by means of artisans."[1] In view, however, of the real purpose of Slöjd teaching, this is but a very secondary consideration.

Inasmuch as it is one of the indirect objects of Slöjd exercises in the schools, to give the pupils a respect for manual work and for those engaged in it, an important consideration is that the pupils are far more likely to look with respect upon what one of their ordinary teachers is engaged in, than upon anything which they are handed over by the teacher to be dealt with by an artisan brought for the purpose from outside.

In Sweden, considerable experience has been obtained of the working of both plans: for ten years artisans were employed to a very large extent; now, in nearly every case, the work is in the hands of ordinary teachers.

III.—DRAWING.

Under the rules of the Commissioners of National Education, Drawing is taught in National Schools in Class III. and upwards, and only as an optional subject; a Results Fee is paid for it, (2s. 6d. in Class III., rising to 5s. in Class VI.), if it be taught by a specially certificated teacher. During the year 1896 it was taught in 1,519 schools; and the number of pupils examined was 74,317, of whom 58,488 passed. The total number of children on whom Results Fees were earned in any subject in the Classes in which drawing may be taught was 574,278, showing that only 12·9 per cent. of the pupils are instructed in Drawing. The number of teachers holding certificates to teach Drawing is 3,827 (1,885 masters and 1,942 mistresses). As Drawing was taught only in 1,519 schools, it would appear that many of the teachers possessing such certificates do not give instruction in the subject. In 1896 there were 11,619 teachers employed in the National Schools, so that at present 29·9 per cent. of the teachers are certificated to teach Drawing.

We find considerable confusion existing as to terms used to denote different branches of Drawing taught in elementary schools. We, therefore, define the meaning in which we propose to use certain terms.

Freehand Drawing.—This term we apply to the reproduction on the same or different scales without mechanical aid, of examples which have been already drawn on the flat.

Mechanical Drawing.—This term we apply to drawings produced by the aid of instruments, whether copies of drawings, plans to scale, conventional representation of solid forms, or the construction of geometrical figures—a form of Drawing often included under the term "Geometrical Drawing."

Model Drawing.—This term we apply to the pictorial representation of solid forms without mechanical aid.

Brushwork.—A modification of Freehand Drawing in which the brush and colour replace the pencil.

Colourwork.—A system of Drawing in which masses are represented by tints of colour.

Drawing in Light and Shade.—The representation in perspective of models or objects with lights and shadows properly depicted.

In practice, we find that in Ireland only Freehand Drawing is taught in the National Schools; frequently no instruction is given, and the children are provided with a copy-book, and left to themselves to copy a drawing already depicted on the left hand page on to the right hand one, whilst their teacher is engaged with some other classes.[2] The only other form of Drawing at all generally practised is the copying in the higher classes of shaded pictures.

---

[1] *The Theory of Educational Sloyd*, by Otto Salomon, London, 1892, page 71.

[2] Evid., vol. I., *Purser*, 544. Evid., vol. III., *Browne*, 11803–5; *Clements*, 13351, 14010–12. Evid., vol. iv., *Br. Thomas*, 14811–3; *Alexander*, 15788; *W. E. Joyce*, 16364.

That the teaching of Drawing under these conditions is not satisfactory, seems to have been universally felt in Ireland, and of the witnesses we have examined the majority strongly desire that the course of instruction in Drawing should be of a more practical nature;[1] that Drawing should be continuously taught from the infants' class onwards, and that as soon as possible a simple course of Drawing should be introduced into all National Schools.[2]

Part II. Section III. Drawing. — Evidence.

In England, Drawing is a compulsory subject in all boys' schools; grants for it are also made in the case of girls if drawing is taught in the upper standards of the schools. In Scotland, Drawing is not a compulsory subject.

Drawing in England and Scotland.

In 1896, Drawing was taught to 2,290,412 children in 20,028 elementary schools in England, Wales, and Scotland.

In England and Scotland, since March, 1898, the Parliamentary Grant for Drawing which had previously been administered by the Science and Art Department is administered by the Education Departments of the two countries.

To earn grants it was necessary that the instruction should be given by a teacher holding a certificate. This certificate could be acquired by passing the examinations held by the Department of Science and Art in certain Art subjects, but the teachers' ability to teach was not tested, the examinations being those open to all Art students.

In the Code of the Education Department for 1890, laid on the table of the House of Commons, and published about March of that year, it was stated in clause 101, that the satisfactory teaching in Drawing of all boys in schools for older scholars in England and Wales would be made a condition of the annual grants of the Education Department which should fall due after the 31st August, 1891. The possession of a Drawing certificate on the part of the teacher was at the same time dispensed with.

The number of schools in which Drawing was taught during the year ending August 31, 1890, was 4,824. During the year 1890-91 it increased to 6,012, and in 1891-92, when the subject was made compulsory, the number was 18,228.

In 1894, the Department of Science and Art decided to issue certificates of capability to teach Drawing for grants in elementary schools to all older teachers, who having taught Drawing in their schools, had obtained two good reports since 1891.

Drawing is taught in elementary schools, receiving grants from the Department of Science and Art, in accordance with a definite syllabus, which lays down the nature of the instruction for each standard within clearly defined lines. Within the last few years an alternative syllabus has been issued, and we find a growing tendency to give to local educational authorities more latitude in framing courses suited to their particular circumstances. The evidence we have received is mainly concerned with the amount of instruction in Drawing that can with advantage be given by the average teacher, and the direction towards which it should tend. It has been pointed out that Drawing can be associated with many subjects of instruction, and that the Mechanical Drawing may generally be practically applied.

We conclude, from the evidence before us, and from the fact that Drawing has been made a compulsory subject of elementary education in most European countries, that practice in careful observation and accurate drawing is a very valuable part of mental discipline.[3]

It is necessary therefore to consider in more detail the results, both utilitarian and educational, of instruction in the various branches of Elementary Drawing; and to ascertain to what extent such instruction can be introduced into all National Schools in the immediate future, bearing in mind the facts, that many of the teachers have not been trained to give instruction in Drawing, and that all teachers cannot be expected to develop artistic ability.

Various branches of Drawing.

Freehand Drawing naturally suggests itself as the basis of all instruction in Drawing that is to be the means of training in accurate observation, and ready representation by a graphic method of what the eye perceives. In drawings from flat copies, the relative

Freehand Drawing.

---

[1] Evid., vol. i., [illegible]. Ibid., vol. ii., Wagner, 4399. Evid., vol. iv., E. J. Alexander, 18870; W. B. Ross, 16976-7; Courtney Clarke, 17427-33.

[2] Evid., vol. i., Moran, 1103-6. Ibid., vol. ii., Mooney, 4831-2; Dr. Kerr, 6402. Evid., vol. iii., Browne, 11389; [illegible], 11817; Holland, 12186; Coffey, 11861; [illegible], 13181, 13485; Heath, 13816; Clements, 14018. Evid., vol. iv., Mr. Thomas, 14601; [illegible], 15030; [illegible], 15804; Robinson, 16940; Courtney Clarke, 17426; [illegible], 18437.

[3] Evid., vol. ii., [illegible], 6516. Evid., vol. iv., [illegible], 18618, 23891-3, 24913-4.

Part II.
Section III.
Drawing.

lengths of lines on the copy and completed drawing are the same; the pupil is therefore not confronted by the difficulties inherent in drawing from solid objects, where the representations of straight lines when correctly drawn on paper are not proportional to the actual lengths of the lines on the object, but vary also according to their inclination to the line of sight of the observer, and where the character and shape of curves vary according to the point of sight.

For study of form, for training in the use and manipulation of a pencil, and in accurate observation, and for cultivation of the power of judging relative distances between points, Freehand Drawing is the simplest branch of Elementary Drawing that can be employed, and the one that can be most easily supervised by an unskilled teacher.

Mechanical Drawing.

Mechanical Drawing is eminently utilitarian, and does not demand from teacher or pupil any skill in the unaided use of a pencil, that cannot be easily acquired. It may, however, be made the means of much useful training and mental discipline. The copying of rectilinear figures by means of the ruler and pencil, but without resorting to measurement, except as a check when the work is completed, is a useful exercise for young children in accurate observation and judgment of relative distances.

Practice in the construction of geometrical figures, is both a mental exercise requiring thought and reasoning, and a training that lays up a store of knowledge that will be frequently useful in after life, and if confined to the more elementary figures is quite within the scope of primary education.

Some knowledge of the conventional methods of representing solids in plan, elevation, and section, or in some other form of projection, forms the fundamental basis of technical training.

The practical application of Mechanical Drawing[1] should be taught to children whenever possible in connection with their other lessons. This may be well exemplified by the use made of drawing in the Hand and Eye exercises and Woodwork; in Cardboard work, the development of a solid (i.e., the shape it would assume if its faces could be laid out on one plane) is drawn, and from the drawing the solid is constructed; again in Woodwork, the plan and elevation, and if necessary a section of an object are drawn, and from these data the object itself is afterwards constructed. Such simple exercises possess many valuable features: the indication that Drawing may be of practical utility is one; the mental exercise involved in picturing a solid form from a conventional drawing, or vice versa, is another highly educational one, and furthermore they lay a basis for further training in industrial occupations.

A power to impart instruction in this branch, within the limits we have indicated, should not be beyond attainment by every teacher.

Model Drawing.

Model Drawing is perhaps the form of drawing which most immediately appeals to teachers and children, but we have received evidence that it is an exceedingly difficult form of Drawing in which to give efficient instruction, and the mere substitution of formulae, derived from the rules of perspective, for the training of the students' eyes as to how to see, destroys many of the advantages of such a form of Drawing.[2] It is however undoubtedly desirable that all children should be taught to make sketches of simple objects, which may at least serve to jot measurements on, and form the basis from which to construct an accurate conventional drawing. The very simplest forms of Model Drawing should therefore be taught in all schools, but great proficiency in the subject can be expected only from schools in charge of teachers trained in this branch of Drawing.

Brushwork, &c.

Brushwork, Colourwork, and Drawing in Light and Shade, are branches of Drawing which may be looked on as extensions of the forms we have already dealt with; they are more especially useful in developing the aesthetic sense and artistic ability of children, they help to brighten and beautify the lives of the scholars, but are liable to misuse in the hands of unskilled teachers, and cannot therefore be generally introduced.

Use of the Blackboard.

For a teacher a certain facility in drawing on the blackboard is almost a necessity if the instruction in Drawing is to be efficient; indeed for effective instruction in many subjects of every day work, such an acquirement is necessary, especially when

[1] Evid., vol. ii., Anss. [illegible]. Ibid., vol. iv., Anss. [illegible].

[2] Evid., vol. ii., D. Taylor, [illegible].

dealing with young children, when a sketch may supplement words and convey an idea much more quickly and correctly than a merely verbal description. In some schools we have found a line of blackboards fixed around the walls at a convenient height for children to draw on them; those pupils who show proficiency are encouraged to use them, drawing on a larger scale and with more freedom than can be attained under ordinary circumstances. Such efforts are useful principally for the distinction they confer on the young draughtsmen and the spirit of emulation they excite.

Part II. Section III. Drawing.

The scope of Drawing.

We consider that instruction in drawing of a nature to afford training in observation, accuracy, and facility in the graphic representation of objects may be given by every teacher who devotes a little time to the study of the subject, and follows a suitable course in freehand and mechanical drawing[1]. The teacher need not possess great ability as a draughtsman, but should be able to sketch intelligently on the blackboard.

In Drawing, as in other forms of practical instruction, the object of the exercise is not so much the completion of a drawing, as the mental and manual training involved in its execution. It is of the utmost importance therefore that the methods of instruction should receive particular attention.

In Freehand Drawing, large charts should be used in addition to the smaller copies now generally to be found in schools, or the teacher may draw an example on the blackboard, adapted for any particular purpose. The children should be carefully taught to estimate the relative distances of points, and their success in so doing may be tested by measurements. The proportion between the various components of the example should be carefully pointed out; and when curves and ornaments are employed as examples they should be analysed on the blackboard, and the method in which the ornament is built up should be explained. The teaching of Mechanical Drawing involves continual explanation of the use of instruments, of the conventions adopted, and of the reasons for the various steps taken. It follows then that, during the lessons in Drawing, frequent instruction must be given by the teacher, and that the lesson should never degenerate into mere unaided copying of examples.

Recommendations.

We recommend that a course of Elementary Drawing should be introduced into all National Schools with the least possible delay: that the course of Drawing throughout should be in continuation of the Kindergarten Drawing; that the course should be continuous and progressive throughout a child's attendance at school; and that Drawing should, as far as possible, be taught in connection with the other forms of practical instruction. The course should comprise both Freehand and Mechanical Drawing in all classes, and in the Fifth and Sixth Classes might include very simple Model Drawing.

In Freehand Drawing, the artistic faculties may, to a certain extent, be cultivated by the selection of examples correct in form, and possessing beauty of line.

The Mechanical Drawing, commencing in the First Class, when only the ruler should be used as an aid, should be gradually developed throughout the classes, and might in the case of rural schools lead up to the representation of buildings, fields, &c., in plan and to scale; and in the case of urban schools, or schools where woodwork is taught, to the representation of simple objects in plan, elevation, and section. The construction of the more simple geometrical figures should be taught incidentally in both cases.

Instruction in Drawing should be an integral part of the training of all teachers attending the Training Colleges. We do not consider that the possession of a certificate of ability to draw is absolutely necessary for a teacher, now engaged in school work, before he is allowed to give elementary instruction as indicated above; but we consider that some proof of ability to give instruction should be required from a teacher before he receives grants for such instruction. We also think that an opportunity of being trained in method and in the use of the blackboard should be available for all untrained teachers.

We consider that Drawing may be further utilised in elementary schools as an aesthetic training; but to be thus utilised it must be taught by a highly qualified person possessed of considerable natural ability.

The artistic abilities and tastes of the students may be cultivated to some extent, and their originality and initiative encouraged by a carefully graduated course of design, in which brushwork and colourwork are used in addition to the pencil. We have seen

[1] Evid., vol. i., *Moran*, 1456–8. Evid., vol. ii., *H. Taylor*, 3346–58.

Part II.
Section III.
Drawing.

very admirable results obtained in the production of designs in colour, each student during a lesson developing a separate design of his or her own invention on general lines laid down for the day by the teacher.

We recommend that when any teacher has received an art training and satisfies the Commissioners of National Education that he possesses the necessary artistic ability, such teacher should be permitted to supplement the Elementary Drawing by introducing art training throughout the classes, in accordance with a scheme, which he should be at liberty to develop according to his own taste, subject to approval by the Commissioners.

We think that every encouragement should be given to such developments, but they should only supplement, and not supersede, the elementary instruction which we have suggested.

Section IV.
Elementary Science.

Definition.

IV.—ELEMENTARY SCIENCE.

We use the term Elementary Science as including the first elements of Natural and Physical Science suitable for schools, but not including Arithmetic, Algebra, or Geometry. As a subject of education Elementary Science is eminently practical, not only because it helps to give an intelligent knowledge of the material world, but also because it has a direct bearing on the arts and industries of modern life. The teaching of it begins with Object Lessons in the Kindergarten classes; and it may be continued all through the higher classes, with the aid of experimental illustration.

Present condition of science teaching.

In Ireland, at present, various branches of Elementary Science are optional subjects for Classes V. and VI., under the Board of National Education. The courses prescribed are of the character in vogue many years ago, being designed rather to teach the results of scientific investigation, than to give any definite kind of mental training. Owing to a number of causes, including the smaller amount of the Results Fees offered by the Board of National Education, teachers have generally preferred to teach this subject in connection with the Science and Art Department. Within the last few years, however, this Department has ceased to pay for second class passes;[1] and in consequence the number of National Schools in which Science is taught under the Department, has seriously decreased. There are now, indeed, so few National Schools which teach any branch of Elementary Science, either in connection with the Board of National Education or with the Department of Science and Art,[2] that this subject may be said to have practically disappeared from the primary schools of Ireland.

In England, a course of Object Lessons, which may be regarded as the first stage of Elementary Science, is compulsory in the lower standards of primary schools; and many schools carry on a course of science teaching into the upper standards. In Scotland, too, considerable progress has been made, of late years, in the same direction. And on the Continent, some form of Elementary Science is almost everywhere compulsory in primary schools.

Evidence received.

We have had evidence before us: (1) On the value of the training to be obtained from Elementary Science; (2) On the proper methods of giving it, and on the importance of adopting such methods; (3) On the interest which the pupils take in it; (4) On the possibility of introducing it into schools without any large expenditure on equipment and on current expenses.

Importance of the study.

(1.) As to the importance of science training, all the witnesses are agreed.[3] The mere fact that some form of it prevails in all kinds of schools in so many other countries outside Ireland, proves the consensus of opinion on the subject; and the fact that it is being more and more widely extended, is sufficient evidence that its importance and value have stood the test of experience. Nearly all the authorities insisted on the teaching of science as an efficient means of training the faculties. They pointed out

[1] Ibid. vol. iii., Purser, [illegible].

[2] Ibid. vol. iii., [illegible], [illegible]. Sixty-third Report of the Commissioners of National Education in Ireland (1896-7), p. 32.

[3] Ibid. vol. ii., Armstrong, [illegible]; [illegible]; [illegible]. Ibid. vol. iii., Arnold Graves, [illegible]. Ibid. vol. iv., Sir Thomas, [illegible]; [illegible]; [illegible].

that it cultivates the powers of observation, and exercises both memory and understanding. The habit of drawing conclusions from facts, and the verifying of these conclusions by observation and experiment, tends to careful and correct judgment. The study of science makes constant appeal to individual reason: the pupil arrives at no conclusion without seeing it to be true; and thus his knowledge becomes more solid and thorough, and he gradually acquires self reliance in testing the accuracy of his observations. Finally, science must be the basis of all successful technical instruction.

Mr. A. E. Scougal, one of Her Majesty's Inspectors of Schools in Scotland, describes very well the educational ends that are attained by the introduction of this branch of work into the school course. He says:

> "I think the place of elementary science is, in the first place, as I have said, to [illegible] [illegible] [illegible] [illegible] [illegible] [illegible] [illegible] [illegible]."[1]

There was a general consensus of opinion as to the valuable effects of science teaching on the intelligence of the children.[2] We found it generally admitted by teachers that the children became quicker in taking in elementary subjects, through their having this science instruction.

Proper methods of teaching.

(2.) As regards the proper methods of teaching science, and the importance of giving it on proper lines, we had a great deal of evidence.[3] The general purport of the evidence may be summarised by saying that "in the teaching of science in elementary schools, instead of scientific facts merely being taught, the children should be rather taught how to find out things for themselves."[4] It was held by all the expert witnesses that Elementary Science ought not to be taught without practical illustrations and experiments, in which as far as possible the pupils should themselves take part.[5] Object Lessons should be used as a means of training the children to ask questions, and to learn from their observation, and not merely for the purpose of giving information.

Interest of children in the study.

(3.) The witnesses were satisfied that the children take a great interest in Elementary Science; and the classes we saw receiving this kind of teaching were evidently delighted with their work. This interest, we were assured, reacts upon the other school subjects, and tends to vivify the whole work of the school.[6]

Cost of equipment.

(4.) There can be no doubt as to the possibility of introducing Elementary Science into primary schools, as this has been done in a very large number of schools in England, Scotland, and on the Continent. The expense of introducing these subjects need not be very large, as was clearly proved by the evidence given.[7] Some expense, of course, is necessary; and the cost of equipment and of maintenance should be provided without calling for any outlay on the part of the teacher.

Recommendations.

We consider that the Board of National Education should determine, with some degree of precision, the general lines to be followed in the teaching of Elementary Science; but that considerable latitude should be allowed, within these lines, as regards the details of the course for each School. Each Manager might be invited to submit, for the approval of the Board, a syllabus of the course which he proposes to adopt. It would be well perhaps, at the outset, if a number of specimen courses, suitable for different classes of Schools, were prepared under the direction of the Board, as a definite guide to Managers and teachers. A system of this kind has already been adopted under the English and Scotch Education Departments.

---

1 Ibid. vol. iv., [illegible].

2 Ibid. vol. ii., [illegible].

3 Ibid. vol. ii., [illegible].

4 Ibid. vol. ii., [illegible].

5 Ibid. vol. ii., [illegible].

6 Ibid. vol. ii., [illegible].

7 Ibid. vol. ii., [illegible].

Part II. Section IV. Elementary Science.

General principles.

The principles that should underlie every course of Elementary Science in primary schools, are these :—(1) The lessons should rather illustrate the general principles of science, than give prominence to any particular branch of science; (2) The method of instruction should be practical and experimental, special importance being attached to careful observation and exact measurement; (3) The pupils should as far as possible perform the experiments themselves, and should learn to devise experiments to test their observations; (4) The courses should include a study of solids and fluids, of simple chemical actions, and of natural classification of plants and minerals. The study of the various subjects should be so combined into a consecutive course as to train the pupils in the fundamental methods of science, and to produce habits of observation, of accuracy, of intelligent inquisitiveness, and of testing observations and explanations.

Object Lessons.

In conducting Object Lessons, the intellectual training to be derived from them must be kept steadily in view. To interest the children in natural objects and phenomena, to train them to observe systematically and to put together and record their observations, these are the ends to be aimed at, and they can only be attained by continual practice. Pictures may be of use in extending the scope of the lesson, and interesting the pupils in matters outside their immediate experience. For example, in an object lesson on a piece of coal, a picture of a coal mine may be introduced to give the pupils interesting information as to matters outside the range of their experience; but this extended interest has a different educational end from the principal one of the lesson, and should not encroach unduly on the latter, and still less be substituted for it. Some teachers have been so anxious to convey general information, by means of these lessons, that they have overlooked the much more important aim, namely the intellectual training. Some have even gone so far as to suggest that when their pupils were being tested by the Inspector, it was not a suitable test if the objects were then present; evidently thinking that the lessons should have filled the pupils with information to be reproduced from memory, rather than have cultivated their ability to study objects intelligently." The obtaining of general information, like the extending of the interests of the pupils beyond their immediate surroundings, is an important but subordinate end of Object Lessons. Being easy of attainment, and more easily tested than the really important intellectual training, there is great danger that the subordinate may be substituted for the more important end, unless continual attention be directed to the true purpose of Object Lessons.

The subjects available for Object Lessons are innumerable: plants and animals; food; manufactured articles; common minerals; natural phenomena, such as rain, snow, wind; simple machines such as pumps, pulleys, hinges; local events, such as the building of a house, harvest operations. In every case, the lesson should be given with the object present. A lesson on snow should be given while snow is on the ground; a lesson on harvest operations, in a harvest field. While subjects of general interest of this kind should not be excluded, still most Object Lessons should be connected with things collected by the pupils themselves or in ordinary use, should serve as helps and preliminaries to the ultimate teaching of science, and should therefore be given in a predetermined order, and with distinct reference to the more advanced science teaching which is intended to be afterwards taken up. The scientific spirit and the scientific method should be present, but should not be obtruded."

Object Lessons should be arranged with special reference to the locality in which the school is situated, and to the circumstances of the children. The chief difference between schools should be as to the objects used. In town schools, for example, the objects would naturally illustrate physical science; in country schools, the natural history of plants and animals. In girls' schools, special prominence might be given to subjects connected with domestic life.

We strongly recommend that Object Lessons in the junior classes, leading on to a more advanced course illustrated by experiments in the senior classes, should be made compulsory in National Schools, as soon as teachers can be sufficiently prepared to give this instruction in the proper way.

Experimental Course.

In the experimental course the pupils should take part in the experiments themselves, as far as possible, and should write out descriptions of what they do and observe, and should be led to generalize intelligently and to test their generalizations by further experiments. Where measurements are made, they should be carefully recorded.

Part II. Section IV. Elementary Science.

and the pupils should make simple diagrams of the apparatus used and of the arrangement of it for the purpose of the experiment. Thus, the teaching of Elementary Science may be made to furnish exercises in composition, in writing, in spelling, in arithmetic, and in drawing; so that it will not be detrimental to the proficiency of the pupils in these subjects, if some time be taken from them for Elementary Science.

Course for Boys.

For boys, the course of instruction in town schools might be framed on the lines of Course H. of the English Education Department[1]. The details may be varied according to circumstances; but care should be taken to keep in view the fundamental idea that underlies it, the pupils being first trained in the method of conducting an investigation, and then led on to apply this method to the solution of a simple but definite problem. In country schools, the course of instruction for boys may be made, with advantage, to include those elementary principles of Science which have a direct bearing on the art and industry of Agriculture, as recommended in the next section.

Course for Girls.

The course of Elementary Science for girls, whether in town or country schools, may be the same as that adopted for boys; and this will often be found convenient in Mixed Schools under one teacher. But, in the larger schools, with more than one teacher, a separate course for girls, having special reference to Domestic Science, may be more desirable in many cases. A detailed syllabus of such a course, drawn up by Mr. Heller, Science Demonstrator under the London School Board, will be found in Appendix A.[2]

Compulsory as soon as possible.

We strongly recommend that a course of Elementary Science on the lines here described in continuation of Object Lessons in the junior classes, be introduced into the higher classes of National Schools in Ireland. When precisely in the school course Object Lessons shall merge into more definite science instruction is a question that will depend on the character of the teacher and of the pupils in each school, and is consequently one of the things in which great latitude should be allowed. This Elementary Science should be made compulsory as soon as teachers can be trained to give it. As this training will require time it should be taken in hand with the least possible delay.

Method of testing.

We desire to repeat, in reference to Elementary Science, what is stated elsewhere in this Report, in respect of other subjects of instruction, namely, that we do not consider that this kind of teaching can be satisfactorily tested by a mere examination of pupils in the form of question and answer, but that for its development along proper lines, it is essential that it be tested by inspection of the methods of instruction employed by the teacher, and by observing his success in interesting the pupils and awakening their intelligence. On the first introduction of these subjects, it will be desirable to provide fully qualified Science Organisers, an important part of whose duty it should be to advise teachers, and to help in drawing up detailed courses suitable for their schools.

Special branches of science.

We consider that instruction in special branches of science should not be given to pupils until they have substantially completed some general course, such as that which has been just described. Instruction in scientific branches would more fitly find a place in "Continuation Schools," to be attended by pupils who have already completed their elementary education. Until such schools are established in sufficient numbers in Ireland, we are of opinion that special branches of science might be taught, as optional subjects, in Class VI. of the National Schools. Care must be taken, however, that this teaching shall not interfere with the general course of Elementary Science now recommended.

V.—AGRICULTURE.

Section V. Agriculture.

So far back as the year 1837, the Commissioners of National Education in their Report for that year expressed their intention of providing for instruction in those branches of science which have a practical application to husbandry and handicraft. We find, however, that at present the branches of science "having a practical application to husbandry" do not hold so prominent a place in the school curriculum as the Report of 1837 would lead us to expect, while practical farming, so far at least as such a subject can be taught from a text book, is one of the chief branches of instruction.

---

[1] Appendix A. XVIII. (1.) (5.)
[2] Appendix A. XVIII. (3.)

Part II. Section V. Agriculture.

Agriculture in the National Schools.

Agriculture is a compulsory subject for boys of the Fourth and higher classes in all rural schools, and it is optional for girls. Even in town schools the subject may be taught to boys and girls. In 1896, the number of pupils examined in it was 88,773, of whom 56,473 passed. The results fees amounted to £13,285.

The programme laid down by the Commissioners of National Education consists of various chapters of a text-book entitled "Introduction to Practical Farming," which deals with such subjects as the following: Cultivation of Land; Manures; Live Stock; Dairying; Gardening; Agricultural Implements; Land Drainage and Reclamation; Farm Fences, &c. The subject is taught in the National Schools, as a rule, entirely from this text-book,[1] and is unaccompanied by any practical illustrations,[2] a knowledge of the textbook alone being required by the rules of the Commissioners.

Evidence received.

The evidence we have received throughout Ireland goes to show that the subject as taught is of little educational value.[3] The children do not get any real grasp of the subject, as no efforts need be made to give them a practical acquaintance with the objects and processes described in the lessons. For example, Dr. T. J. Alexander, Head Inspector of National Schools in Cork, states that the "present book teaching is worthless."[4] Mr. Purser, another Head Inspector, expressed the same opinion.[5] Lord Monteagle, who is much interested in agricultural education, is of opinion that "the present teaching out of a book is wholly useless, if not worse."[6] Similar evidence was given by many other competent witnesses.[7]

This opinion is quite in accordance with the evidence we received in England. Mr. John Chalmers, Head Master of Burton School, Westmorland, stated that he would not think anything of a system of teaching agriculture merely out of books.[8] Mr. James Bateman, Organising Secretary to the Westmorland County Council, was of opinion that mere text-book teaching of agriculture was useless.[9] Another witness, Mr. G. Courtenay Hodgson, Organising Secretary to the Cumberland County Council, was of opinion that theoretical instruction without work by the pupils on an experimental plot was quite valueless.[10] Mr. T. G. Rooper, one of Her Majesty's Inspectors of Schools in England, declared that he would never encourage the teaching of agriculture merely from books.[11]

Recommendation.

Moreover, we are strongly of opinion that even if the instruction were more efficiently given, the subject of Practical Farming forms no fitting part of the programme of a primary school. The details of the art of Agriculture can only be learned by practice on a farm and by pupils who are, as a rule, beyond the usual primary school age. The attempt to teach these details theoretically to children of school age can be of little profit. As regards the scientific aspect of Agriculture on the other hand, some preliminary training in the simplest elements of Natural and Physical Science is absolutely necessary for a proper appreciation of the bearing of scientific principles on the practice of farming. While therefore we fully recognise the great importance, especially as regards Ireland, of instruction in Practical Farming, we consider that this should be given only in special schools of a technical character.

We are, consequently, of opinion that the course in Agriculture at present prescribed for National Schools, should be altered. The new course should consist of instruction in the elements of the Natural and Physical Sciences that have a direct bearing on Agriculture; and this instruction should be given with the aid of experiments of a simple character, performed as far as possible by the pupils themselves. Such a course of instruction will be of a nature entirely within the capacity of the children of a primary school. It will afford a good disciplinary training for all children, even for those who

---

[1] Ibid., vol. i., A. Alexander, 308; Purser, [illegible]; [illegible]. Ibid., vol. iii., [illegible], 16489. Ibid., vol. iv., [illegible]; [illegible]; [illegible]; [illegible]; [illegible], 21278.

[2] Ibid., vol. i., A. Alexander, 318; Purser, 788.

[3] Ibid., vol. iii., [illegible]. Ibid., vol. iv., Dr. [illegible]; [illegible]; T. J. Alexander, 13178; [illegible]; [illegible]; [illegible]; [illegible]; [illegible], 21217.

[4] Ibid., vol. iv., 20718.

[5] Ibid., vol. i., 785.

[6] Ibid., vol. iv., 18716.

[7] Ibid., vol. ii., Armstrong, [illegible]; [illegible]. Ibid., vol. iii., [illegible]; [illegible]. Ibid., vol. iv., Dr. Thomas, [illegible]; Monteagle, [illegible]; [illegible]; Professor Wallace, [illegible]; [illegible].

[8] Ibid., vol. ii., 8972.

[9] Ibid., 2043.

[10] Ibid., 8330-1.

[11] Ibid., 5497-8.

are not to be subsequently engaged in the practice of agriculture, while it will enable those who are to be so engaged, at a later stage to make intelligent use of scientific treatises on the subject. Part II. Section V. Agriculture.

The course in Agriculture, thus modified, will naturally constitute the course in Elementary Science for boys in rural schools.[1]

In this connection we beg to draw attention to the following extract from a publication recently issued by the French Government on the "Teaching of Elementary Ideas of Agriculture in Rural Schools,"[2] which clearly expresses our views on the subject:— French scheme for teaching elementary agriculture.

"Instruction in the elementary principles of agriculture, such as can be properly included in the programme of primary schools, ought to be addressed less to the memory than to the intelligence of the children. It should be based on observation of the everyday facts of rural life, and on a number of simple experiments appropriate to the resources of the school, and calculated to bring out clearly the fundamental scientific principles underlying the most important agricultural operations. Above all, the pupils of a rural school should be taught the reasons for these operations, and the explanations of the phenomena which accompany them, but not the formulae of methods of execution, still less a manual of maxims, definitions or agricultural precepts. [illegible] and this can be done only by the experimental method.

"[illegible]

"[illegible]

"The work of the elementary school should be confined to preparing the child for an intelligent [illegible]."

We publish as an Appendix[2] a translation of the French official publication referred to above, embodying a scheme based on these principles. We are of opinion that such a scheme, suitably modified, should be introduced into Irish rural schools. It might with advantage be supplemented by a course involving calculations of areas and volumes from actual measurements, and in the higher classes, very simple mapping of fields and roads, from the pupils' own observations. The pupils should be encouraged to make collections of natural objects for themselves and for the schools, to observe the injuries done by fungi and insects, and to keep small gardens of their own either in a school plot or in the neighbourhood of their own homes.

There are 41 National Schools having farms attached varying in area from 1½ acres to 35 acres, in which instruction is given not only in the theory but in the art of practical agriculture. These farms are technically known as "School Farms." The Commissioners of National Education, as a rule, have no property whatever in them; they belong either to the school patrons, managers, or teachers. School Farms.

Special fees are paid for the proficiency in Agriculture of the pupils of these schools and for the satisfactory condition of the farms. These fees amounted in 1896 to £681 5s. 8d. Payments are also made to certain of the pupils for working on the farms, to agricultural monitors for superintending the pupils, and to the teachers for training the agricultural monitors.

As the object of the School Farms is to teach Practical Farming, we do not consider that they should permanently receive aid from the Board of National Education. Aid might, however, continue to be given by the Board to existing farms, pending the establishment of a complete system of Agricultural Education in Ireland. School Gardens.

There are also 69 National Schools having gardens attached, usually less than one acre in extent, in which instruction is given in cottage gardening, poultry management, &c. These are known as "School Gardens."

Special fees are paid, as in the case of the School Farms, for the proficiency of the pupils in Gardening and for the satisfactory condition of the gardens. These fees amounted, in 1896, to £249 19s. 6d.

---

[1] See page 58.

[2] Appendix D.

Part II. Section V. Agriculture.

In order to give teachers facilities for experimental teaching, we recommend that School Gardens, each of which need not be more than one rood in extent, should be provided, where possible, in connection with rural schools. These gardens if well and tastefully kept, would have a refining and elevating influence on the children, and would thus indirectly tend to improve the surroundings of their own homes. Even where land is not available for School Gardens, the teacher should endeavour by simple experiments in the schoolroom to illustrate natural processes, such as the germination of seeds, the effect of manures, &c., and should utilise any opportunities afforded by the locality to exemplify the practical applications of scientific principles. In connexion with this, the French scheme referred to above, will be found to contain many useful suggestions.

Agricultural Training Establishments.

The Commissioners of National Education have two Agricultural Training Establishments—the Albert Agricultural Institution at Glasnevin, County Dublin, and the Munster Dairy Farm and Agricultural Institute, near Cork. In both, instruction is given in the science and practice of Agriculture, Dairying, &c. The only direct connexion that these establishments have with the primary schools is that National Teachers attend classes of agricultural teaching at the Albert Institution, and the students from some of the Dublin Training Colleges also attend lectures there. No pupils of National Schools attend either institution. Paying students are received at both of them, but a certain number of free places are offered for competition every year.

The Albert and the Munster Institutions are both doing excellent work, especially as regards Dairy instruction; but as technical training in Agriculture does not seem to us to be a subject that properly belongs to a system of primary education, we consider that these institutions should be handed over to some department having special charge of agricultural education. By a department of this kind the usefulness of such institutions might well be developed and their number increased. Arrangements, however, should be made by which both these establishments would still be available for the instruction of National School teachers in the sciences having a direct bearing on Agriculture, in so far as this cannot be sufficiently provided for in the Training Colleges.

Section VI. Cookery, &c.

VI.—COOKERY; LAUNDRY WORK; DOMESTIC SCIENCE.

COOKERY.—We regard Cookery as a most important branch of Practical Instruction. It is of special importance in Ireland where the labouring and artisan classes are sadly ignorant of the art of Cookery, their food in consequence being seldom prepared in as economical or nutritious a manner as it might be.

Besides, the evidence we have had in England and Scotland in reference to Cookery shows the attractiveness of the subject to the pupils, and its usefulness in securing greater regularity of attendance, and in encouraging the pupils to stay on longer at school.[1]

Cookery in the National Schools.

According to the latest returns, viz., those for 1896, Cookery was taught in 83 National Schools in Ireland. 1,724 girls were examined in this branch, and 1,535 passed.

Before that year, the instruction in this subject had been carried on exclusively by members of the regular school staff, who either held certificates of competency or were regarded by the Commissioners of National Education as sufficiently qualified. Owing to difficulties arising from cost of appliances, expense of materials, and want of suitable accommodation, the instruction made but little progress. It was taken up in very few of either the Ordinary National Schools or the Model Schools, and may be said to have been confined to the Convent National Schools and to the Practising Schools of the Training Colleges for females.

In 1893 the Commissioners of National Education obtained from the Government leave to engage some special itinerant teachers of Cookery and Laundry work. The sanction was given only as an experiment, and the number of teachers for whose employment provision was made, was limited to four. The teachers to be employed were persons who were trained in these branches under the Royal Irish Association for Promoting the Training and Employment of Women, and who, at the close of their course of training, had undergone an examination and obtained from the National Union for the Technical Education of Women, diplomas of competency to teach. Part II. Section VI. Cookery, &c.

These teachers travel through the country, remaining for a sufficient time at selected centres, and giving instruction in various National Schools in the district, one or more lessons of two hours being given in each school each week. The course embraces twenty Demonstration and Practice Lessons in Household Cookery suitable for National School pupils of Classes IV., V., and VI. The necessary room for the purpose is provided by the manager of the school, who also arranges for the supply of materials, and for such appliances as the special teachers may find necessary in addition to what they bring with them.

We are of opinion that this useful subject should be encouraged in the schools. Instruction might in many cases be given by special teachers in Centres[1] where the classes could be attended by the pupils of schools in the immediate neighbourhood; in others the instruction in this subject must be given by the ordinary school teachers. In the latter case special provision must be made for the training of the teachers by itinerant teachers or otherwise. We consider that the teaching of this subject should be continuous, not in the sense that it should be taught every day, but that it should be taught to one or more classes each week, throughout the year or a considerable part of it. We are of opinion that only plain Cookery should be taught; and that the appliances should be simple and mainly such as the pupils will have in their own homes. This branch may be successfully taught in ordinary schoolrooms, when not otherwise occupied, and with the simplest appliances. Recommendations.

It is now felt that such a subject as Cookery, useful as it is even if taught in a mechanical way, may become still more useful if made to aid the general course of education. The practical lessons should be supplemented by lessons in theory, and both should be interdependent.

The scientific principles underlying the subject should be explained and illustrated by experiments, as a part of the object lessons and other science lessons in the school.[2] The importance of accuracy in weighing and measuring should be insisted upon; the blackboard should be used for the writing out of directions; the reasons of the processes should be explained; and the children should write notes of the lessons, and a statement of the results of their work. These notes should be carefully revised by the teacher, and bad handwriting, incorrect modes of expression, and errors in spelling, should be pointed out and corrected. The course should include demonstration lessons in which the processes should be gone through and explained by the teacher, and practice lessons in which the same processes should be gone through by the pupils. During the demonstration simple lectures should be given, dealing with all points of the subject; e.g. the current prices of provisions, the cost of a meal, the methods of selecting meat. The efficiency of the instruction should be tested by occasional visits of the Inspector whilst the classes are being taught, and in such other way as the Commissioners of National Education may determine.

We would refer especially to the account of our visit to the Central School at Bethnal Green, London, for a somewhat detailed statement of the manner in which lessons in Cookery may be effectively given.[3]

Laundry Work.—In Ireland Laundry work has only recently been recognised by the Board of National Education as a school subject, and is taught as yet in but very few schools. Laundry work in the National Schools.

When in England we inquired particularly into the systems of teaching Laundry work in the elementary schools, and we obtained much interesting information. We may refer especially to the systems in use under the London School Systems adopted in England.

---

[1] See pages 36, 37.

[2] Evid., vol. ii.; [illegible]

[3] Appendix A., VII.
See also Appendix A., XXI., Scheme of Instruction in Cookery, etc., under School Board for London; Appendix A., XXV. (3), Syllabus of Cookery Lessons for Elementary Schools; Appendix A., XXX. (4), Course under Barrow-in-Furness School Board.

Part II. Section VI. Cookery, &c.

Board and the Barrow-in-Furness School Board. Under the London School Board, Laundry work is an obligatory subject for girls in the higher standards. A lesson is usually of two hours' duration, one hour being devoted to a demonstration by the teacher, and one hour to practice by the pupils. The course consists of eleven lessons, one lesson being given each week for eleven weeks.[1] In Barrow-in-Furness, there is an excellent scheme of Laundry work instruction.[2] There is one marked difference between the system in Barrow and that in London. In London the instruction is given by one lesson a week until the course is finished. In Barrow the course consists of ten consecutive lessons, and a class of fourteen goes through the entire course in one week, attending morning and afternoon. Both in London and in Barrow, the "Centre" system[3] is adopted for teaching Laundry work.

Recommendation.

We recommend the encouragement and extension of instruction in Laundry work. The instruction should proceed on lines similar to those which we have laid down in the case of Cookery. The circumstances of the schools and of the districts in which they are situated, will determine whether the course should be one of consecutive lessons, as in Barrow-in-Furness, or of lessons given at intervals, as in London.

The account of our visit to the Bethnal Green Centre, referred to above, will be found to contain useful information on instruction in Laundry work.[4]

Domestic Science in the National Schools.

Domestic Science.—The course laid down by the Commissioners of National Education comprise certain portions of special text-books on Domestic Economy and Hygiene. These are recognised as extra subjects, and may be taken by girls in the Fifth Class and upwards. The courses extend over two years, and the examinations are confined to testing the pupils' knowledge of the contents of the text-books under such heads as the following, viz., in Domestic Economy:—Food; Clothing; Cleanliness; The Dwelling; Simple Ailments; and in Hygiene:—Air; Breathing; Ventilation; Water; Alcoholic Liquors; Food.[5]

In 1896 Domestic Economy was taken up in 151 schools in which 1,979 pupils were examined, and 1,026 passed; and Hygiene in 39 schools, in which 650 pupils were examined, and 374 passed.

Recommendation.

The acquiring of information on such subjects from text-books is useful, but it is still more necessary that a power of applying this information should be gained. Such power can only be gained by a thorough knowledge of the principles involved, such as can be obtained from actual experimental observation.

The theoretical portion of the subject should be studied by means of lessons well illustrated by experiments, which if possible should be performed by the children themselves. These lessons should commence with a preliminary training in accurate measurement, and they should include the following:—A study of the laws of gases in general, especially the atmosphere and its composition, leading to the principles of ventilation and causes of contamination; some knowledge of the theory of heat, and of the effects of heat on organic matter; a study of water, its chemical composition, the causes of hardness, and power of solution; the chemistry of the more simple substances used in the household; a study of the materials of clothing, and the effects of heat, water, &c., on them; the outlines of Human Physiology, breathing, digestion.

From such instruction, which would form a suitable course of elementary science for girls, the same educational results may be looked for, as have been more fully described in the section of our report dealing with Elementary Science.

A good example, in our opinion, of the kind of course in Domestic Economy and Hygiene that should be given in a girls' school may be seen in Appendix A.[6]

Housewifery.

We found during our visit to London, that practical application of Domestic Economy, under the name of Housewifery, has been recently introduced by the School Board.

---

1 Evid., vol. iii., Miss Harrison, 6304. For Syllabus see Appendix A, XXI. (6).
2 Evid., vol. iii., Miss Andrews, 16340–16435. For Syllabus, see Appendix A, XXX.
3 See pages [illegible].
4 Appendix A, VII.
5 *Rules and Regulations of the Commissioners of National Education in Ireland* (June, 1896), p. 72.
6 Appendix A., XVIII. (B).

In the one institution that came under our notice—viz., in the Central School at Bethnal Green, London,—the method employed was said to work successfully. Part II. Section VI. Housewifery, &c.

The following extract from the evidence on this subject of Mrs. Homan, Member of the School Board for London, and Chairman of the Domestic Subjects Committee of the Board, will show the continuous and interesting character of the experiment:—

> "We have, wherever we possibly can, four small rooms, consisting of a kitchen, a small sitting-room, a small bedroom, and scullery, so as to represent, as far as possible, a workman's small dwelling, and the girls are taught to do the whole of the work of the house in proper order, and with proper method; that is to say, they are taught to do the whole week's work, and they do it in a methodical, proper manner; they are also taught a great deal of the theory upon which it is based, and they have illustrated lessons given them in the class, with books upon which they take notes, and have examinations on the blackboard, and questions, and so on, and have notes of lessons, as well as doing practical work."[1]

We also found at our visit to the Loreto Convent National School at Bray, near Dublin, that Housewifery had been introduced there about ten years ago. It is carried out on a smaller scale than in the Bethnal Green Centre, and exclusively at the expense of the Loreto Community, as the subject has not yet been recognised by the Commissioners of National Education. We were informed that the subject has proved both useful and attractive to the senior girls.

While we are of opinion that Housewifery can seldom be introduced as a subject of instruction in National Schools, still, so far as it is practicable, it is undoubtedly useful, and provision should be made for it in the Rules of the Commissioners of National Education. Recommendation.

VII.—NEEDLEWORK: SPECIAL INDUSTRIES.

From the foundation of the system of National Education in Ireland, provision was made for the instruction of girls in needlework; but the precise amount of time to be devoted to this branch was not fixed prior to 1863. In the year 1863, the Commissioners decided that the minimum time to be devoted to needlework, &c., should be one hour daily; and the existing rule is:— Section VII. Needlework, &c. Needlework in the National Schools.

> "That instruction shall be given in plain needlework in all Schools in which Female Teachers or Workmistresses are employed; and that in all such Schools, every girl in classes in which needlework is required to be taught, shall receive instruction in needlework for at least one hour on each of the five school days of the week, unless on application of any Manager the Board may, for special reasons, dispense with this rule in his School."[2]

The Commissioners provide[3] that in a mixed school (i.e. for boys and girls) conducted by a master, in which there is no female assistant, a Workmistress may be employed, during two hours daily, when there are at least twenty girls in average attendance. Workmistress.

The ordinary course of needlework instruction extends from the Second to the Sixth Class inclusive. In the lower classes it comprises hemming and knitting, plain patching and darning, making pinafores, cutting patterns of plain shirts or of articles of girls' underclothing, crochet, &c.; and, in the Sixth Class, it requires proficiency in the different branches of plain sewing and knitting.[4] Ordinary course.

In their Report for 1896 the Commissioners state that, during that year, 17[illegible] girls were examined in needlework, and that 161,263 passed.[5]

In the year 1889, the Commissioners introduced, for girls of the Sixth class attending National Schools in which a female teacher was employed, a new programme,[6] in which the industrial course of instruction was made more advanced than that previously in operation in the Sixth Class, while the literary course was reduced in extent. "The Alternative Scheme."

Feeling, however, that difficulties might arise in some localities in the adoption of the new programme, the Commissioners provided that should any manager, for special reasons, apply for exemption from it, his school might be exempted[7]; and they state in

[1] Evid., vol. ii., Mrs. Homan, [illegible].
[2] Rules and Regulations of the Commissioners of National Education in Ireland (June, 1896), p. 1.
[3] Ibid., p. 30.
[4] Ibid., pp. 49-[illegible].
[5] Sixty-third Report of the Commissioners of National Education in Ireland, p. 16.

Part II. Section VII. Needlework, &c.

their Report for 1896 that it was found, at the close of that year, to be carried out by 1,487 schools, representing only about one-third of the schools in which it might possibly have been taken up.

The requirements of the combined literary and industrial programme, styled, in the Commissioners' Rules for 1890, the "Alternative Scheme for girls of Sixth Class," were as follows:—

Literary Programme.

Reading (which should include Text Books on suitable Industrial subjects, such as Domestic Economy), with knowledge of the subject matter;

English Composition, including Letter Writing on various subjects, which should embrace Geography, Grammar, &c. [illegible]

Industrial Programme.

Plain Needlework (in its various developments, including Dressmaking). This must be one of the three industrial subjects to be taken up daily in each of the two years of a Sixth Class Course.

Subjects in Classes A and B (as below), any two of which may be adopted at the choice of the Manager, and within the capacity of the Teacher.

Class A.—1. Dressmaking (plain); Underclothes making. 2. Plain Upholstering; Baby Clothing. 3. Knitting and Crocheting of Jerseys, Caps, Wraps, Vests, Petticoats, Socks, Stockings, Gloves, Slippers, and similar articles. 4. Good repairing of garments, bed linen and table linen, &c., such as darning (damask and knitted), fine-drawing, patching, re-seating, refooting, re-knitting, heeling, cutting; also plain [illegible]. 5. [illegible], Children's Cloaks and [illegible], Little Boys' suits, [illegible]. 6. [illegible] washing, carding, spinning, and weaving of wool. 7. Treatment of flax and weaving of linen.

Class B.—1. Lace-making—Youghal, Limerick, Carrickmacross, [illegible], or other recognised kind. 2. Mountmellick Work—Embroidery (on Handkerchiefs, &c.), ornamental marking of linen. 3. Art Needlework, including Embroidery from Celtic patterns. 4. Gold and Silver Lace Work—Ecclesiastical Embroidery. 5. [illegible] Embroidery. 6. Glovemaking. 7. Artificial Flower making. 8. Basket-making—[illegible]; Straw Hats, Straw plaiting, &c.; other articles produced from Straw or Wicker. 9. Other kinds of Cottage Industries, such as Wood Carving, Net Mending, where local or suitable.

When introducing this new programme for Sixth Class girls, the Commissioners addressed an explanatory memorandum on the subject to the managers and teachers of National Schools, in which, in reference to girls who had satisfactorily passed the two stages of the Fifth Class, they expressed the opinion that the industrial or practical part of their education, although fairly advanced so far, was yet manifestly susceptible of large and important extension, and stated that they resolved that girls who had passed the two stages of Fifth Class should devote the remainder of their school life mainly to industrial education so as to prepare them for the practical duties of their homes, or for employment in profitable industries.

To carry out this idea, it was arranged that about two hours a day of the ordinary school hours should be devoted by the Sixth Class girls to plain Needlework and special industrial branches.

Recommendations.

We consider that the requirement of an hour a day for needlework in the classes generally is excessive, and we suggest that the minimum time set apart for this subject should be three hours a week. From what we have seen in English schools and from the inquiries we have made we are satisfied that three hours a week is quite sufficient. The proposed introduction of other subjects of practical instruction is an additional reason why less time than at present should be devoted to Needlework.

There is great danger of Needlework becoming mechanical.[1] The evidence of Sir Joshua Fitch, on this point, is deserving of careful consideration :—

> "Needlework is a very useful art as we all know, but it is an art that children may sit and dawdle over for many hours in a state of complete mental vacuity; there is extremely little in needlework, as commonly taught, to draw out intelligence or inventiveness, or mental effort of any sort."[2]

To guard against this danger special attention should be paid to the educational side of the subject, and, to this end, the work should be varied, and, where possible, frequent demonstrations on the blackboard should be given.

As regards the "Alternative Scheme," we consider that the two hours a day devoted to industrial instruction under this Scheme is excessive, and that many of the subjects

---

[1] Evid. vol. ii., *Fitch*, [illegible]; *[illegible]*, [illegible]. Evid. vol. iv., *E. M'C. Murray*, [illegible].
[2] Evid. vol. ii., *Fitch*, [illegible].

included under it are unsuited to primary schools. We therefore think that this scheme should be discontinued. We are, however, of opinion that the first four subjects in Class A of the scheme, viz.:—Dressmaking (plain); Fine Underclothing; Knitting and Crocheting of Jerseys, &c.; Good repairing of garments, hose, &c., should be taught as extra subjects, either within, or outside of, school hours. Part II. Section VII. Needlework, &c.

In the case of a mixed school conducted by a master, in which there is no female assistant, we are of opinion that an average attendance of twelve girls should warrant the appointment of a Workmistress. We also consider, especially as no pension is attached to the position, that the present rate of remuneration of Workmistresses—£12 a year—is quite inadequate.

Special Industrial Departments are recognised in connection with certain National Schools,[1] if the managers desire that special provision be made for the instruction and training of monitors, as well as of female pupils who have passed through the Sixth Class, in Embroidery and other advanced kinds of Needlework, or other approved branches of industrial instruction for females. A salary, dependent upon the circumstances of the case, is awarded to a Special Industrial Teacher thoroughly qualified to organise and conduct such instruction. This Teacher is charged with the special supervision of the entire industrial education in the school, including the Plain Needlework, &c., prescribed in the programmes of the several classes; but the recognition of a Special Industrial Teacher does not relieve the ordinary female teachers of the school from the obligation of giving efficient practical instruction, under the supervision of the Special Industrial Teacher, in Plain Needlework, &c., to the pupils of the school classes. Special Industrial Departments.

The number of these Departments on December 31, 1896, was sixty-one.

We consider that the only subjects of an industrial character with which the Commissioners of National Education should have to do are those, such as simple dressmaking, cookery, &c., which form an essential part of a girl's education, having regard to the efficient discharge of her household duties. Recommendation.

At present, however, other subjects of an industrial character are taught in some of these departments, such as:—Art Needlework, Bookbinding, &c. Similar subjects, such as Net-mending, Weaving, Dairy Management, Poultry-keeping, Bee-keeping, are taught under the head of "Cottage Industries."[2] We are of opinion that instruction in these subjects, and provision for industrial employment would more properly fall within the scope of a special Department of Industries.

VIII.—SINGING.

Section VIII. Singing.

We have already referred to the large part played in the Kindergarten by Singing and by rhythmical movements of various kinds.[3] We regard these as essential elements in a scheme of complete education for older children as well as for infants.

Singing is recognised in the programme of the Board of National Education as an optional subject, for which a result fee, varying from 1s. 6d. to 3s. in the different classes from the second to the sixth, may be paid. In the year ended December, 1896, the number of pupils examined in Singing was 75,842, in 1,817 schools; and a sum of £7,559 was paid on account of 49,287 passes. Singing in the National schools.

The Report of the Commissioners for 1896-7 states that the Tonic Sol-fa method is now generally adopted by managers. This method is so simple that by means of it very young children can be taught to sing by note. Indeed, instances are of frequent occurrence where the power of singing by note is acquired by children to some extent before they have learned to read. The method admits, moreover, of easy gradation; it proceeds in accordance with strict educational principles, the practical application of which it admirably illustrates; and it can be made the means of introduction to even the highest forms of music.[4] It is shown by the experience of many schools, both in this country and in England and Scotland, that by means of this method even junior classes can be brought to sing from notation at sight, and to regard this not as a difficult task The Tonic Sol-fa method.

[1] Rules and Regulations of the Commissioners of National Education in Ireland (Edition 1898), pp. 6-7.
[2] Ibid., p. 73.
[3] See page 18.
[4] Reid, vol. i., Mins. Evid., 9683-87; Goodman, 13938-39.

Part II. Section VIII. Singing.

but as a pleasant exercise. To the pleasure derived from singing—such as might be had from singing by ear—there is added the pleasure of conscious mastery over a new form of expression.

We think that having regard to the simplicity of the Tonic Sol-fa method, there should be but few teachers who could not with some little trouble acquire a practical knowledge of it so as to be able to use it profitably in the instruction of their pupils. It ought to be regarded as part of the normal function of the teacher in a primary school to teach the elements of vocal music to the pupils, and the school in which vocal music is not taught should certainly be the exception.

Official figures: [illegible]

It is to be regretted that up to the present the contrary has been the case in Ireland. The official figures showing the extent to which Singing is taught in the elementary State-aided schools of England and Scotland on the one hand, and in the National schools of Ireland on the other, are instructive in two respects. Whilst they indicate how backward in this respect the National schools of Ireland still are, they also plainly show that Singing may readily be made a subject of very general, and indeed practically universal, instruction in primary schools.

For the year ended in 1896, the official figures[1] are as follows:—

—	[illegible]	[illegible]	[illegible]	[illegible]	[illegible]	[illegible]	[illegible]
							£
England,	[illegible]	[illegible]	[illegible]	4,4[illegible]	4,[illegible]	[illegible]	[illegible]
Scotland,	[illegible]	[illegible]	[illegible]	[illegible]	[illegible]	[illegible]	[illegible]
England and Scotland,	[illegible]	[illegible]	[illegible]	[illegible]	[illegible]	[illegible]	[illegible]
Ireland,	[illegible]	[illegible]	[illegible]	[illegible]	[illegible]	[illegible]	7,[illegible]

Restrictions in force in Ireland.

In considering these figures, two points are to be borne in mind. In both England and Scotland, the grant for Singing—reduced, however, by one-half—may be earned by a school in which Singing is taught, not by note, but by ear only. Again, in neither country is it required as a qualification for the teaching of Singing, that any special certificate of competency to teach it shall be held by the teacher. In both respects, the regulations in force in the National Schools of Ireland are altogether more stringent: in the Irish National Schools singing by ear is not recognised at all, and no teacher can become entitled to a grant for the teaching of Singing who does not hold a certificate of competency to teach it. Such a certificate is to be obtained by passing an examination in a course prescribed by the Commissioners of National Education, the percentage required for passing the examination being 50 per cent.

[1] The returns from which the figures are taken are, in each instance, the latest as yet available ([illegible]). For England, the figures are those of the year ended [illegible]; for Scotland, they are the figures of the year ended [illegible]; for Ireland, they are the figures of the year ended [illegible].

In each case, the figures regard **only the schools that were actually inspected, for the purpose of the** State grant, within the year.

It may be useful to observe that, as regards both England and Scotland, the "average attendance" indicated by these official figures is not the actual average attendance in the schools in question, but is the result of a computation, and is described in the official returns as the "average attendance for payment," that is to say, it is the attendance as calculated for the purposes of the State grant.

In England, for [illegible], the computed "average attendance" was [illegible] above the actual average attendance for the year; and in Scotland, for the same year, the computed "average attendance" exceeded the actual average attendance by [illegible]. In England, and to some extent in Scotland, the excess of the computed over the actual average attendance arises from the fact that in both countries the attendance of pupils in the class commonly known as "half-timers" is reckoned on a somewhat liberal principle, each attendance, within certain limits, being counted, in the case of such pupils, as an attendance and a half. (See the English Education Code for [illegible], art. [illegible]; and the Scotch Code for the same year, art. [illegible].) In Scotland, a similar allowance is furthermore made in the case of all pupils who reside "two miles or upwards from a suitable State-aided school." (See the Scotch Code for [illegible], art. [illegible].)

It is obvious that the general introduction of the teaching of Singing in the National Schools of Ireland is not to be hoped for until these restrictions are relaxed. The detailed statistics published in the annual Reports of the English and Scotch Education Departments make it plain that the present widespread extension of Singing in the Elementary Schools of England and Scotland has come about through a gradual process of transition,—singing by ear having at first held a position of great prominence, from which it has gradually been displaced by the substitution of singing by note. As regards England, this is fully illustrated by the following figures:—

Sec. II. Section VIII. Singing.

Report of existing Grants.

Years.	Number of Schools or Departments: Inspected during the year.	In which Singing was taught.	In which Singing was taught by note.	In which Singing was taught by ear.	Average number of pupils	Number of Pupils.* [illegible]	[illegible]	[illegible]	Percentages of Pupils. [illegible]	[illegible]	[illegible]
[illegible]	[illegible]	[illegible]	[illegible]	[illegible]	[illegible]	[illegible]	[illegible]	[illegible]	[illegible]	[illegible]	[illegible]
[illegible]	[illegible]	[illegible]	[illegible]	[illegible]	[illegible]	[illegible]	[illegible]	[illegible]	[illegible]	[illegible]	[illegible]
[illegible]	[illegible]	[illegible]	[illegible]	[illegible]	[illegible]	[illegible]	[illegible]	[illegible]	[illegible]	[illegible]	[illegible]
[illegible]	[illegible]	[illegible]	[illegible]	[illegible]	[illegible]	[illegible]	[illegible]	[illegible]	[illegible]	[illegible]	[illegible]
[illegible]	[illegible]	[illegible]	[illegible]	[illegible]	[illegible]	[illegible]	[illegible]	[illegible]	[illegible]	[illegible]	[illegible]
[illegible]	[illegible]	[illegible]	[illegible]	[illegible]	[illegible]	[illegible]	[illegible]	[illegible]	[illegible]	[illegible]	[illegible]
[illegible]	[illegible]	[illegible]	[illegible]	[illegible]	[illegible]	[illegible]	[illegible]	[illegible]	[illegible]	[illegible]	[illegible]

The same process of transition from singing by ear to singing by note has been in progress in Scotland. In Scotland, however, throughout the period covered by the above table, singing by ear has held a much less prominent place than in England. Taking the latest available figures—those for 1895–6,—we find that in that year, the grant in Scotland was paid on 537,201 pupils for singing by note, and on only 58,280 for singing by ear, representing percentages of 91·16 and 8·84, respectively: the corresponding percentages for England, in that year, being 80·77 and 14·29.

The grants for Singing.

Incidentally we may here point out that the principle on which the grants for the teaching of Singing are paid in the Elementary Schools of England and Scotland is altogether different from that on which these, as well as all other grants for the teaching of special subjects, are paid in the National Schools of Ireland. In Ireland, all such payments are made exclusively in the form of Results Fees, the amount to be paid to each school depending upon the number of pupils who individually pass an examination held by the Inspector. But in England and in Scotland, the payments are made as capitation grants, so that the amount payable to a school is regulated, not by the results of an individual examination of the pupils, but by the average attendance of pupils in each class in which Singing is satisfactorily taught.

The Results System.

We have elsewhere referred* to the amount of time which the Inspectors in Ireland are at present obliged to devote to the mere work of examination, and to the extent to which they are thus hampered in the discharge of other obviously important duties of their office. We feel bound to point out that a widespread extension, such as we contemplate, of the teaching of Singing in the National Schools of Ireland, would seriously aggravate this disadvantage, unless a system such as that on which the grants are paid in England and in Scotland be substituted for the system of individual examination and payment by Results Fees, which is still maintained in Ireland. It is important here to observe, that in the official instructions to Her Majesty's Inspectors of Elementary State-aided Schools in England, under the head "Instructions as to Examination in Singing," the first instruction given to the Inspectors is that "the music-tests are not to be applied to individual children."

* In consequence of a difference in the form in which the official returns were issued, it is not possible to include in the table the figures for the years preceding 1882–3.

† It will be observed that, from 1882–3 onward, the figures are given for every third year only.

‡ As singing by ear is much rarer in the larger than in the smaller schools, the number of pupils singing by note is relatively much greater than the number of schools or departments in which singing by note is taught.

* See page 54.

Part II. Section VIII. Singing.

Progress.

As we have made special reference to the Tonic Sol-fa method, it seems not out of place to add that one of the most notable series of figures in the official returns for England and Scotland is that which records the steady continuous increase in the adoption of this method in the schools of both those countries. The closeness with which the transition from singing by ear to singing by note corresponds with the continually increasing adoption of the Tonic Sol-fa method in the schools, is eminently worthy of notice.

The figures for England are as follows:—

Year.[1]	Number of Schools or Departments				
	In which Singing was taught.	In which Singing was taught by Ear.	In which Singing was taught by Note.	In which the Tonic Sol-fa Method was adopted.	[illegible]
1883–4,	21,581	14,348	9,243	6,779	2,475
1884–5,	22,248	11,886	10,382	8,178	2,184
1885–6,	23,548	12,620	11,028	8,887	2,188
1886–7,	24,856	12,083	12,767	10,642	2,104
1889–90,*	26,571	13,694	12,897	12,889	2,284
1892–3,	29,761	9,656	20,106	17,665	2,422
1895–6,	30,684	7,404	23,280	20,478	2,869

Thus, in England, where, in the twelve years from 1883–4 to 1895–6, there has been an increase of 14,032 in the number of schools or departments in which Singing is taught by note, there has been, within the same period, the almost identical increase of 13,699 in the number of schools or departments in which the Tonic Sol-fa method is followed.

So, too, in Scotland, from 1885 to 1896, the number of schools or departments in which Singing is taught by note has increased from 1,740 to 2,509, an increase of 769; and within the same period the number of schools or departments in which the Tonic Sol-fa method is adopted has increased by the closely corresponding number of 697.

Recommendations.

We regard these facts as pointing clearly to the conclusion that if singing by ear be recognised as a subject for a grant in the National Schools of Ireland—as it has for so many years past been recognised in the elementary State-aided schools of England and Scotland,—the working of the Tonic Sol-fa method may be relied upon to bring about the gradual, and even speedy, introduction of singing by note as a general subject of instruction in Irish National Schools. But it will rest with the Commissioners of National Education to make such regulations as will ensure that the recognition of singing by ear shall not become the occasion of introducing into the schools anything unworthy of the name of music, or calculated to hinder rather than help the advancement of the pupils to a higher form of vocal training.

Section IX. Drill, &c.

IX.—DRILL AND PHYSICAL EXERCISES.

Drill and Physical Exercises are recognised as subjects of instruction under the Board of National Education, in connection with Kindergarten.

Present position in Ireland.

Such exercises form a prominent feature in the training of children on Kindergarten methods, and in National Schools where Kindergarten occupations are taken, the younger children are taught [2] "to sing action songs, and go through calisthenic

[1] See page 48, footnote 1.

[2] See page 48, footnote 1.

exercises and simple Kindergarten games."[1] But out of the 8,6[illegible] National Schools in operation in 1898, the Kindergarten system was practised in only 357, so that in the vast majority of National Schools, there is no official recognition of any kind of physical training. In a few instances we have found managers encouraging such training in their schools, but the great mass of the pupils in the Irish primary schools receive no training in this useful branch of practical education. Part II. Section IX. Physl., &c.

In England and Scotland, we found that considerable attention is paid to the physical training of the children in the primary schools. The children in the Kindergarten classes receive systematic instruction in those simple and pleasant exercises which have for their object the development and strengthening of the body, and the training of the mind to habits of order and prompt obedience. But such instruction does not cease when the children leave the Kindergarten classes. It is carried on throughout the Standards, and the older scholars, both boys and girls, have the advantage of this training all through their school life. It is to be noted, too, that the highest grant for discipline and organisation will not be paid to any school in England or Scotland, in which provision has not been made in the time table of the school for some form of Drill or suitable Physical Exercises[2]. In England and Scotland.

Almost every European country has its own system of school Drill, and the subject is considered so beneficial that it is compulsory in most elementary schools. It is evident from the reports we have received, that the subject is regarded as most valuable in itself, and as affording a pleasant variation in the work of the day. On the Continent of Europe.

It cannot, we think, be denied that the physical training of school children, both boys and girls, is of great importance. It makes them alert and orderly, trains them to hold themselves erect and to walk properly. It is especially desirable in towns, where bodily training in games, garden-work, and out-door occupations can rarely be obtained by children of the working classes. For girls, both in town and country schools, it is particularly needed. Such training is no additional burden on school life. On the contrary, it is found from experience that it increases the attractiveness of the schools, and provides a welcome variety of occupation. Besides this, it develops physical strength, and the children return from it to their literary work with renewed zeal and energy.[4] Advantages.

But in addition to systematic Drill and Physical Training, much good can be accomplished by insisting on the children being orderly in their movements in the school-room when moving from place to place, from class to class. The advantages of such a discipline are well described by Sir Joshua Fitch:—

> "You will gain much in a school by cultivating the habit of order and exact obedience about little things. There are right and beautiful ways, and there are clumsy and confused ways, of sitting down at a desk, of moving from one place to another, of handling and opening books, of giving out pens and paper, of entering and leaving school. Petty as each of these acts is separately, they are important collectively, and the best teachers habitually reduce all these movements to drill, and require them to be done simultaneously and with mechanical exactness. Much of this drill is conducted in some good schools by signs only; not merely because it is easy so to economise voice and save power, but also because it makes the habit of instantaneous obedience easier. And children quite sympathise in what is orderly, always like rhythm, and delight in it."[5]

A system of school-room Drill such as is indicated in the above quotation, will induce habits of regularity and obedience, and consequently will be a great aid towards efficient organisation and discipline in the school.

---

[1] *Rules and Regulations of the Commissioners of National Education in Ireland* ([illegible], 1898), p. 66.

[2] Under the heading "Schedule for Discipline and Organisation of &c., &c., &c.," the Circulars of the English Education Code which have been in force for some years past, are as follows:—

"The Departmental grant [illegible] which, if earned, at these rates, shall be paid after considering the report and recommendations of the Inspector.

"The Inspector, in determining which of the higher or the lower of these grants, will have special regard to the quiet [illegible] and conduct of the children, to the neatness and order of the school premises and furniture, and to the proper classification of the scholars both for teaching and examination. . . . The Inspector should also satisfy himself that the teacher has not unduly pressed those who are dull or delicate in preparation for examination at any time of the year.

"The higher grant for discipline and organisation will not be paid to any school in which provision has not been made in the approved Time Table for instruction in Swedish or other drill, or in suitable physical exercises; but children employed in [illegible] and attending school half-time and children for whom such instruction is unsuitable may be excepted."

[4] [illegible]

[5] *Lectures on Teaching* by J. G. Fitch, M.A., LL.D., Cambridge University Press, p. 96.

Part II. Section IX. Drill, &c. — Recommendations.

We accordingly are of opinion that it is most desirable that some simple form of Drill and Physical Exercises should be encouraged in all schools under the Board of National Education; and we think that such encouragement might be most fittingly given in the form of a grant for discipline and organisation, one condition of awarding the grant being that some approved and systematic instruction in Drill and Physical Exercises is regularly and efficiently given.

Part III.

PART III.

COLLATERAL CHANGES IN OTHER PARTS OF THE EDUCATIONAL SYSTEM OF THE NATIONAL EDUCATION BOARD.

The development of Manual and Practical Instruction in the primary schools under the National Education Board, in accordance with the recommendations we have made, will involve certain changes in other parts of the educational system of the Board. Time must be found for the teaching of the new subjects, teachers must be trained to teach them, and provision must be made to secure the harmonious and efficient working of the new subjects and the old in one organised system. We have carefully considered this question, and we feel that our task would be incomplete, if we did not here point out what the changes are which, in our opinion, will be necessary for the purposes referred to, and how these changes may best be carried out. The changes required may be considered in reference to the following:—(I.) Programme of Instruction in National Schools; (II.) Methods of Examination and Inspection of National Schools; (III.) Training College Courses; (IV.) Provision for special training of Teachers in charge of Schools; (V.) Provision for the Association of Schools and of School Managers; (VI.) Evening Schools.

Section I.

I.—CHANGES IN THE PROGRAMME OF INSTRUCTION IN NATIONAL SCHOOLS.

The introduction of the subjects of manual and practical instruction which we recommend, will render necessary some modifications in the existing Programme of Instruction for pupils in National Schools.

School hours.

The Commissioners of National Education lay down in their Regulations that not less than four hours per day must be provided on the Time Table for the ordinary regular business of the school, but that this may include a play-time of not more than half-an-hour. As a rule, however, schools are kept open for about an hour longer than the minimum time. This additional hour is usually devoted to the teaching of extra subjects.

Compulsory subjects.

At present Reading, Writing, Arithmetic, and Spelling, are compulsory subjects for all the classes; Grammar and Geography for the third and higher classes; Needlework for girls in the second and higher classes, and Agriculture for boys in rural schools in the fourth and higher classes.

For various reasons, an increase in the length of the school day is scarcely practicable, and, therefore, in order to make time for the introduction of Manual and Practical Instruction, a modification of the present school programme becomes necessary. The evidence which we have received from English sources shows that such a modification can be effected without injury to the educational interests of the pupils.

Some of our recommendations will make but little extra demand upon the time of the school. In schools in which Agriculture is at present taught, the time hitherto given to that subject will be available for the teaching of it in the new form. Again, our recommendations as regards Needlework imply a reduction of about two hours a week of the time now allotted to that branch. This time will be sufficient for the teaching of Domestic Science.

Recommendations.

For the introduction of other subjects which we recommend, time must be found. The time thus required, which we estimate at not more than three or four hours a week, might be saved (1) by making some subjects, such as Grammar and Geography, optional in some of the classes in which they are now compulsory; (2) by grouping together subjects which are naturally related, instead of assigning to each a separate fragment of time in the time-table; (3) by reducing the requirements of the programme in Grammar, Geography, and Arithmetic.

With regard to this last suggestion, we have received a great deal of evidence that tends to show that Grammar and Geography are at present taught with much greater minuteness of detail than is necessary or desirable in primary schools,* and we are strongly of opinion that, if some of this unnecessary detail were omitted, the amount of time devoted to these subjects might be safely reduced. We have had evidence also, that the course in Arithmetic contains many things that are of little practical use,* and we recommend that it be somewhat abridged by the omission of some of the higher rules. At the same time we recommend that the teaching be made more useful by increased attention being paid to mental arithmetic, and by the introduction of practical questions involving measurement of length, area, and volume.

It should be borne in mind that the time taken for practical subjects will not be entirely lost to the literary subjects, as in many cases, practical instruction implies a certain amount of literary teaching.

We also feel satisfied that the introduction of the subjects of practical instruction into the present curriculum will result in such a general training of the mental as well as of the physical powers of the pupils, that the instruction in the other subjects at present included in the programme of the Board of National Education, will be rendered far more effective. Finally, we are of opinion that as a further result of the changes we have recommended, children, when they have left school, will be in a far better position for self instruction and improvement than they would be under the present system.

II.—CHANGES IN THE METHOD OF EXAMINATION AND INSPECTION OF NATIONAL SCHOOLS.

At the outset of our Inquiry we received important evidence* that the introduction of subjects of manual and practical instruction would necessarily involve a substantial change in the present method of testing the instruction given in the schools. It is therefore necessary to describe briefly the system of examination and inspection of primary schools, which prevails at present in Ireland.

National Schools are examined for Results fees once a year, but incidental visits are made whenever the Inspectors can find time and opportunity. On account of the amount of time taken up by the examinations for Results fees, these incidental visits are necessarily rare. The Results Examination consists in the testing of the pupils in all the subjects taught in the school; and from their answering the efficiency of the school is mainly judged. The pupils who have not made 100 attendances are not examined, and, so far as they are concerned, there is no definite test of the value of the instruction they receive, except that which may be applied by the Inspector when making an incidental visit. Fees are paid to the teacher for each pupil passed at the Results Examination, the amount payable being assessed by a necessarily laborious process in the Education Office, on the basis of the returns furnished by the Inspectors.

The Results Fees system, under which a considerable portion of the teacher's income is dependent on the individual answering of the pupils, was introduced into Ireland in 1871–2; it had been in operation in England for ten years previously.

In England, the examination of the pupils for the purpose of assessing the grant was at first confined to Reading, Writing, and Arithmetic, but this was found unsatisfactory in practice, inasmuch as the range of work tended to become more and more restricted to these subjects alone. Consequently in 1867 a small payment not depending on the number of passes, was made to those schools in which subjects other than the "three R's" were taught in the higher classes. In 1875 these extra subjects were differentiated into "Class" and "Specific" subjects. The former were subjects such as Grammar, Geography, History, which admitted of being taught according to a graduated programme, in all the classes of the school. Payment for these subjects was not made on the basis of individual passes, but according to the proficiency of the class as a whole. Specific subjects were more advanced subjects, such as Mathematics, Languages, Domestic Economy, taken, as a rule, not by whole classes, but by selected pupils in the highest classes. Payment for these subjects was made on the result of individual examination. In 1882 the number of obligatory subjects was increased, and while individual examination in the "three R's" was still insisted on, a Merit Grant was also provided for, to be paid according to the condition of a school or class as a whole, the special difficulties of the teacher, owing to local circumstances, &c., being taken into consideration. In 1890, this system was superseded, and "Class" examination or examination by sample was, except in the case of specific subjects, made the test of school work. Since 1893, in schools which have maintained for a sufficient time a standard of work "well above the level of inefficiency," examination of the pupils has largely been replaced by inspection of the teaching. In other cases a "sample" or "class" examination may still be held if the Inspector is not satisfied with the state of the school after a formal inspection.

In Scotland the mode of examination as a basis for payment of grants has undergone a very similar modification. In that country, payment by results, even in the case of the "three R's," was not introduced till 1873, and from the very first, certain other subjects, viz., those referred to above as class subjects, were paid for according to the success of the class as a whole. As early as 1886, class examination was applied to the "three R's" also, but in the case of children in classes under VI. only. In 1890, individual examination in the "three R's" was abolished in all the classes, except for the purpose of granting labour certificates. In the Scotch Code of the present year, changes have been introduced which are intended to have the effect of combining inspection of methods in the classes generally, at visits without notice throughout the year, with an individual examination of pupils in or beyond Standard VI., towards the end of the school year. On this examination, merit certificates will be awarded which shall attest *individual* proficiency in the whole range of a primary school. It should be explained that no Results fee attaches to these individual examinations, though their collective result may be an element in determining the rate of grant to be paid to a school.

The Results Fees system when introduced into Ireland undoubtedly had beneficial effects on the general character of the work then done in the National Schools. But evidence has been given to us of the benefits that have resulted from the successive changes made in the English and Scotch Educational Systems,[1] whereby the system of individual examination has been gradually replaced by one of inspection; and whilst the scope of our Commission seems to prevent us from expressing an opinion upon the general question as to whether a similar modification might not with advantage be made in Ireland, we consider that as regards the practical subjects of which we recommend the introduction, such a change is absolutely essential. To secure the best effects from Manual and Practical Instruction, the Inspectors should be at liberty to test the progress of the pupils by more flexible methods than can be applied under a rigid system of individual examination. Time should be available for frequent incidental visits. Experience has shown that, even in reference to the present subjects of the programme, this cannot be obtained so long as the existing system is maintained.

III.—CHANGES IN THE TRAINING COLLEGE COURSES.

In order that subjects of manual and practical instruction should be efficiently taught in the National schools, it is clearly of the utmost importance that the students in the Training Colleges should be carefully trained in the best methods of teaching these subjects.

There are at present five Training Colleges in operation in Ireland in connection with the National Education Board, and [illegible] have been granted for the establishment of two other Colleges.

There are two courses of instruction in each Training College—a one-year's course for teachers already classed and in charge of schools, and a two-years' course for other candidates, who have not charge of schools. All the students are called Queen's Scholars.

Each Training College has attached to it one or more Practising Schools, in which the teachers practise the art of teaching under competent supervision, and acquire a practical knowledge of school organization and method.

---

[1] Evid. vol. ii., [illegible]; vol. iv., [illegible].

Part III. Section III.

Course of Instruction.

The course of instruction embraces the following compulsory and optional subjects:—

COMPULSORY SUBJECTS. For Men.	COMPULSORY SUBJECTS. For Women.	OPTIONAL SUBJECTS. For Men and Women.
Reading.	Reading.	Vocal Music.
Penmanship.	Penmanship.	Latin.
Spelling and Punctuation.	Spelling and Punctuation.	French.
English Grammar.	English Grammar.	Irish.
English Composition.	English Composition.	History of Great Britain and of Ireland.
Geography.	Geography.	Trigonometry.
English Literature.	English Literature.	Domestic Economy and Hygiene.
Arithmetic.	Arithmetic.	Practical Cookery.
Book-keeping.	Book-keeping.	Elementary Mechanics of Solids and Fluids.
Theory of Method.	Theory of Method (including Kindergarten).	Magnetism and Electricity.
Practice of Teaching.	Practice of Teaching.	Inorganic Chemistry.
Drawing.	Drawing.	Botany.
Algebra.	Needlework,	Sound, Light and Heat.
Geometry.	and either	Physiography.
Mensuration.	(a) One of the following Subjects:—	
Agriculture,	Algebra.	
and either	Geometry.	
(a) Manual Training, or	Mensuration.	
(b) One of the other Optional Subjects of the Programme.	Agriculture, or	
	(b) One of the other Optional Subjects of the Programme.	

To pass the examination, a Queen's Scholar must obtain 50 per cent. of the gross total of marks allotted to the prescribed subjects, and 30 per cent. of the marks assigned to each of them.

With a view to the introduction of Manual and Practical Instruction into the schools, we consider that with the least possible delay the obligatory course in the Training Colleges should be extended so as to include:— Recommendations.

For Men.	For Women.
Hand and Eye Training, and Woodwork.	**Hand and Eye Training.**
Elementary Science.	**Elementary Science.**
Vocal Music.	**Cookery and Laundry Work.**
	Vocal Music.

In the teaching of Method, the educational considerations which should regulate the mode of teaching the various subjects of practical instruction in National Schools should be fully dealt with, special attention being paid to the principles of the Kindergarten system in reference to the work of both male and female teachers.

In order to give the Queen's Scholars a full course of instruction in methods of teaching we think it most desirable that every subject which is to be taught in any of the Training Colleges should also be taught in the Practising Schools attached to it.

It is evident that the introduction of these new subjects into the course will render necessary substantial modifications in the existing programme for the Training Colleges. We feel that it is no part of our function to indicate in detail how these modifications should be carried out; this must necessarily devolve upon the Board of National Education, but the following are some of the ways in which it may be effected:—

1. By reducing, in some measure, the requirements of the programme in reference to certain subjects.
2. By reducing the number of subjects, failure in any one of which entails loss of the examination by the Candidate.
3. By reducing the number of compulsory subjects for students who have shown sufficient proficiency in these subjects at the entrance examination.
4. By modifying the character of the examination, so as to test rather the capacity of the Queen's Scholars for the work of teaching than their mere knowledge of the various subjects of examination.

Part III. Section IV.

IV.—PROVISION FOR THE SPECIAL TRAINING OF TEACHERS IN CHARGE OF SCHOOLS.

The modification of the Programme of the Training Colleges will not of itself meet all the requirements of the case if Manual and Practical Instruction is to be effectively introduced into the school curriculum within a reasonable time.

Untrained teachers.

At the end of 1896 there were [illegible] Principal and Assistant Teachers employed in National Schools, and of these [illegible] or [illegible] per cent. were untrained. Owing to age or other causes, a large number of these untrained teachers will never be able to enter a Training College, and many of those that could avail themselves of the advantages of a course of training will find it impossible to obtain admission, owing to the keen competition for places and the limited accommodation in these institutions.

Existing provision for training teachers.

In the existing Colleges there are places for [illegible] students, and when the two new Training Colleges are opened, there will be places for [illegible]. But only a small proportion of these places is filled by teachers in charge of schools. The majority of students in Training Colleges are young persons who have not yet held appointments as Principal or Assistant Teachers.

The reduction in the total number of untrained teachers must, therefore, of necessity be a slow process, as it depends on the number of Queen's Scholars annually trained, whether (a) teachers already in charge of schools; or (b) other Queen's Scholars appointed to vacancies previously filled by untrained teachers.

During the three years ended 31st December, 1896, there were [illegible] vacancies in schools, or an average of 683 a year; but there were only 773 trained Queen's Scholars, or an average of 257 a year, available to fill them.

No doubt with the opening of the two new Colleges already alluded to, the number of teachers trained annually will be increased, and ultimately the supply of such teachers to fill vacancies will be less inadequate than it is at present. But for many years to come there must still remain a great number of untrained teachers in charge of schools. Moreover, a considerable percentage of the teachers already trained will require a special course before they can undertake to teach the subjects of Manual and Practical Instruction dealt with in this Report.

Recommendations.

Some provision must therefore be made for the special and speedy training of teachers. Several important suggestions have been made by witnesses[1] as to the best means of effecting this object. Of these the following seem to us the most suitable:—

1. That teachers should attend short courses at the Training Colleges or elsewhere.
2. That classes should be established in the various localities throughout Ireland, at which, on Saturdays, teachers wishing to be instructed in the methods of teaching these special subjects, might be able to attend; the instructors of such classes might be employed, during the other days of the week, as peripatetic teachers or organisers, whose duties would be to visit the schools, to give practical demonstrations, and to advise the ordinary teachers as to the subjects to be introduced, and the best methods of teaching them.

The circumstances of particular cases must determine which of these courses ought to be adopted. Whichever it may be, arrangements should be made, as is at present the case with teachers coming up for a course of Agricultural instruction at the Albert Institution, Glasnevin, enabling the teachers to have the benefit of this special training free of expense. Special grants should also be made to defray the cost of this training, whether given in the Training Colleges or elsewhere.

Section V.

V.—PROVISION FOR THE ASSOCIATION OF SCHOOLS AND OF SCHOOL MANAGERS.

We have been much impressed by the evidence we have received as to the important advantages that may accrue from the association of schools for educational purposes, especially in reference to subjects of manual and practical instruction.

The "Centre" system.

In most of the places which we visited in England we found that instruction in Woodwork and Domestic Science was conducted on the system known as the "Centre" system. A room and suitable equipment, together with a special teacher, were provided in a Centre for the use of a number of neighbouring schools. This room was in constant use all the week round, both in the morning and afternoon. Drafts of

[1] [illegible]

children from the schools thus associated had the use of the rooms and appliances in turn, and each draft received instruction from the special teacher.

Part III. Section V.

Peripatetic Instructors.

There is another system also which we found in operation in Liverpool, in which only peripatetic Science Instructors were provided for groups of schools. These instructors visited each school in turn, bringing with them a supply of suitable apparatus for their demonstrations. In the intervals between the visits of the peripatetic teachers, the ordinary teachers went over the work, by way of repetition, and thus practically the continuity of the instruction was maintained.[1]

These systems, in addition to their other manifest advantages, have the great merit of economy, the money provided for education being much more effectively applied than if expended separately on the various schools.

Recommendations.

We are of opinion that the "Centre" system could be carried out without much difficulty in the large towns in Ireland for instruction in Woodwork, Elementary Science, Cookery, and Laundry work. In the rural districts these subjects will have to be taught in the schools; and if the ordinary teachers are not competent to give the instruction, the peripatetic system might advantageously be adopted.

We are strongly convinced of the advantage of having associations of managers' formed in Ireland for the development of Manual and Practical Instruction, in accordance with one or both of the plans outlined. These associations would be also most useful for the purpose of suggesting changes in the school programme, suitable to particular localities, of promoting healthy rivalry between different schools, and of arousing local interest in educational matters generally.

VI.—CHANGES IN REGARD TO EVENING SCHOOLS.

Section VI.

The importance of Evening Schools, in connection with subjects **of manual and** practical instruction, is everywhere admitted.

Present regulations.

Evening Schools are recognised in Ireland in connection with Model, Convent, Monastery, and Ordinary Day National Schools, or as separate and independent National Schools. The Commissioners grant salaries and Results fees to the teachers of these schools. In the case of Convent and Monastery Schools the salary is a Capitation Grant at the rate of only £10 per annum for every 100 pupils in average attendance—or at the rate of 2d. per month for each pupil. As Evening Schools are open for only six months as a rule, the Capitation Grant is really only 1s. per head for six months' instruction. In the case of Ordinary National Schools the salary is at the somewhat higher, but still quite inadequate, rate of £1 per month for every month during which the school has been open with an average monthly attendance of not less than twenty-five *bona fide* Evening School pupils (that is, pupils who do not attend any Day School). This represents a maximum payment of nearly 5s. per head for each pupil in average attendance for six months' instruction. The teachers of Model Evening Schools are paid at rates somewhat higher than these.

Results fees are granted to all Evening Schools, but subject to **the following** restrictions:—

(a.) Of the ordinary branches, only Reading, Spelling, Writing, Arithmetic, **and** Book-keeping may be paid for.

(b.) Only two Extra Branches can be taught and paid for.

(c.) If Extra Branches are paid for, no payment can be **made for ordinary** subjects for the same pupils.

(d.) Music and Needlework cannot be paid for—but "Sewing Machine and Dressmaking" may constitute an Extra in Girls' Evening Schools.

(e.) No day school pupil may be presented for examination in an Evening School.

(f.) If the pupils have been examined twice in Sixth Class, only Extra Subjects can be paid for.

(g.) Every pupil presented for examination **must have made at least fifty** attendances.[2]

As might be expected, in view of the small remuneration to the teachers of Evening Schools by way of salaries or Capitation Grants, and the restriction on the earning of Results fees, we find that the number of Evening Schools has been decreasing from year to year, and that on the 31st December, 1886, there were only 85 such

[1] Evid., vol. ii., Dublin, [illegible]; [illegible]; [illegible].

[2] Evid., vol. iv., Most Rev. Dr. O'Dwyer, [illegible]; [illegible]; Monsignor Byrne, [illegible]; [illegible]; [illegible].

Part III. Section VI.

schools in operation in the whole of Ireland, and that the average attendance was only 1,147. This is a very striking and unsatisfactory condition of things, when compared with England, where the average attendance at Evening Schools during the same year was 117,048, or Scotland, where the average attendance was 56,822.

In England and Scotland.

In England and Scotland, Evening Schools are encouraged by the State as much as possible, and local effort is enlisted on their behalf by regulations calculated to make such schools attractive and suitable to the requirements of each locality. All hindering restrictions are removed, the programmes are wide and elastic, and the method of assessing the grants is simple.

In both these countries, subject to slight modifications, grants may be made for any of the following subjects of instruction, or for any other subjects that may be sanctioned by the Education Department, provided a graduated scheme for teaching any such subject be submitted to the Inspector and approved by him:—

Elementary Subjects (Reading, &c.)	Subjects for Girls and Women only (Domestic Economy, Needlework, Cookery, Laundry, &c.)
English (including English, Geography, History, &c.)	Drawing.
Languages.	Manual or Technical Instruction.
Mathematics.	Suitable Physical Exercises.
Science Subjects.	Military Drill (Boys and Men).
Subjects of Practical Utility (Book-keeping, Shorthand, &c.)	Vocal Music.
Subjects for Boys and Men only (Agriculture, Navigation, &c.)	

The annual grant is paid according to the total number of hours' instruction given to each pupil who has given at least twelve hours' attendance. There is no formal examination of the schools—but they are regularly inspected.

Objects of Evening Schools.

One object of Evening Schools is to supply defects in the elementary instruction of pupils. In spite of all efforts to the contrary, there must necessarily be a large number of pupils who are unable to spend sufficient time at the ordinary Day Schools, to acquire reasonable proficiency in the elementary subjects. This is especially the case in Ireland, where the compulsory clauses of the Education Act of 1892, have, for various reasons, been put in force in but few places.

Again, these Schools enable pupils who have passed through the ordinary Day Schools to acquire something more than elementary knowledge, and give them opportunities of learning the scientific principles which underlie the employment on which they have entered. As stated by the late Sir Patrick Keenan at the Social Science Congress in 1861, it should be kept in mind that "it is precisely when the rudimentary education ends at thirteen or fourteen, that some effort should be made to induce youths to cultivate themselves, to become readers and students, to observe the phenomena of nature, and to recognise the application of science to their trades and callings."

Evening Schools would in many cases be particularly suitable for manual and practical instruction. Such subjects would undoubtedly render the school attractive. We found in Dundee, for example, that manual instruction in Evening Schools is so popular that it acts as an inducement for pupils to attend the literary classes, no pupil being allowed to attend the manual classes, who does not attend literary instruction as well.

Recommendations.

We are of opinion that the present restrictions upon the payment of grants for pupils attending Evening Schools in Ireland, which so much hamper their operation, should be removed.

We also recommend that the number of subjects which may be taught should be largely increased. Managers of schools should be at liberty to suggest, for the approval of the Board of National Education, any subjects that they consider specially adapted to the circumstances of the locality.

We consider that the system of individual examination is entirely unsuitable to Evening Schools, and that the payments of all the grants should depend (a) on the attendance, and (b) on the efficiency of the school as reported on by the Inspector.

We are also of opinion that the remuneration of the teachers of Evening Schools in Ireland is entirely inadequate, and that it should be increased to such an extent as would fairly reward the teachers for their labours, and obviate the necessity of requiring school fees from the pupils to supplement their incomes.

In presenting this Report to your Excellency, we venture to express our conviction that, if our recommendations be adopted, the system of education carried out in the primary schools of Ireland can be made, within a few years, very thorough and complete. At present, no doubt, it is excellent in some respects; but in other respects it seems to us seriously deficient. Insisting too much, as it does, on the study of books, it leaves the faculty of observation and other important faculties comparatively uncultivated; and it neglects almost entirely that training of the hand and eye which would be so useful to the children in their after life, and which is now regarded, both in England and on the Continent of Europe, as an element of great importance in primary education.

The development of Manual and Practical Instruction, on the lines we have pointed out, will remedy these defects, and will not, we are satisfied, inflict any injury on the literary education which is now given. It will not disturb what is good in the present system, but only supply what is wanting. It will quicken the intelligence of the children, brighten the tone of school life, and make school-work generally more interesting and attractive. With the system of National Education enriched as we propose, the children will be taught not by means of books only, but also by the more simple and effective agency of things; they will be trained in the skilful use of all their faculties; and they will be better prepared for their work in life, which, for the great bulk of them, must consist mainly of manual occupations.

It is hardly necessary to say that the changes we have recommended cannot be carried out without a considerable expenditure of money. But we feel confident that the State, which so largely maintains and controls the system of National Education in Ireland, will not hesitate to provide the necessary funds for improving that system, within reasonable limits. The progress of the people in wealth and material prosperity must largely depend on the education given in the primary schools; and to make that education thoroughly efficient and fit for its purpose is a task, we submit, which may well be undertaken, in the highest interests of the State, whatever the necessary cost may be.

At an early period in the progress of our Inquiry, we had the misfortune to lose by death one of our most valued colleagues, His Grace the Most Rev. Edmond Lord Plunket, late Archbishop of Dublin. The great desire of His Grace for the advancement of education in Ireland, and his acquaintance with the educational needs of the country, fitted him in an especial manner to take part in the work entrusted to us; and we feel it our duty to place on record our deep sense of the loss we sustained by his death.

The Earl of Belmore, Chairman of the Commission, attended our meetings most assiduously during the whole progress of our Inquiry, guiding our proceedings and taking part in our discussions. He was also present at meetings in December, January, and February last, when the substance and general outline of this Report were unanimously agreed to. After these meetings, we regret to say, he became seriously indisposed, and has not since been allowed by his doctors to transact any business in connection with the Commission.

We desire, in conclusion, to bear testimony to the zeal and efficiency of our Secretary, Mr. J. D. Daly, in the discharge of his duties. To his intelligence, his diligence, and his courteous manner, we are indebted for much valuable assistance, both in the holding of our Inquiry and in the preparation of our Report.

All which we humbly submit for your Excellency's consideration.

Signed this 25th day of June, 1898.

✠ WILLIAM J. WALSH,
Archbishop of Dublin.
C. PALLES.
C. T. REDINGTON.
JAMES J. SHAW.
GERALD MOLLOY.
HENRY EVANS.
H. B. WILSON.
GEO. FRAS. FITZGERALD.
STANLEY HARRINGTON.
WILLIAM ROBERT J. MOLLOY.
T. B. SHAW.
J. STRUTHERS.

JAMES DERMOT DALY,
Secretary.

ALPHABETICAL LIST OF WITNESSES WHO GAVE EVIDENCE BEFORE THE COMMISSION.

Name.	Description.	Volume and Page of Minutes of Evidence.
[illegible], John [illegible]	Member of the Education Committee of the [illegible] County Council.	IV., 351, 381
[illegible], G. W., M.A.,	Clerk to the Glasgow School Board,	IV., 319
Alexander, T. J., M.A.,	Head Inspector of National Schools,	IV., 41
[illegible], Arthur, [illegible]	Assistant to the Professor of Agriculture, Yorkshire College, Leeds,	III., 1
[illegible], Miss A.,	Laundry Work Instructress to the [illegible] School Board,	II., 340
Armstrong, Henry E.,	Professor of Chemistry, City and Guilds of London Institute,	II., 36
[illegible], S.,	Head Master, Model School, Carrickmacross,	IV., 319
Barrett, W. F., F.R.S.,	Professor of Physics, Royal College of Science, Dublin,	IV., 410
[illegible], Richard, J.P.,	Vice-President of the Governors of the Munster Dairy School,	IV., 12
[illegible]	Organiser of Manual Instruction to the School Board for London,	II., 69
[illegible]	District Inspector of National Schools,	IV., 48
[illegible], James,	Organising Secretary to the Westmoreland County Council,	II., 262
[illegible]	Hon. Secretary to the Governors of the Munster Dairy School,	IV., 19
[illegible] H.,	One of the Governors of the Munster Dairy School,	IV., 2
[illegible], H. S., LL.D.,	District Inspector of National Schools,	IV., 216
[illegible], Arthur E.,	One of Her Majesty's Inspectors of Schools in England,	II., 224, 250
Bevis, A. W.,	Director of Manual Training to the Birmingham School Board,	II., 1
Blair, Robert, M.A., B.Sc.,	Inspector of Schools under the Science and Art Department,	IV., 285
[illegible], A. T., B.A.,	Senior Inspector of Schools to the Liverpool School Board,	II., 179
[illegible], J. B.,	National Teacher, [illegible] National School, County Limerick,	IV., 83
[illegible], Miss Margaret,	Mistress of the Infant Department, [illegible] Bridge School, Edinburgh,	IV., 283
[illegible]	Head Master, Dublin Metropolitan School of Art,	III., 60
[illegible], Robert,	National Teacher, [illegible] National School, Belfast,	IV., 163
[illegible], W. A., B.A.,	District Inspector of National Schools,	III., 138
[illegible], W. J., B.A.,	District Inspector of National Schools,	IV., 225
[illegible], O. A., M.A.,	Senior Inspector of Schools under the Science and Art Department,	II., 99
[illegible], Colonel [illegible], D.L.,	Deputy Lieutenant, Co. Tyrone,	IV., 193
[illegible], Rev. Brother,	Superior, Christian Brothers' Schools, North Monastery, Cork,	IV., 33
[illegible], Wm., B.Sc.,	Agricultural Instructor to the Trustees of the [illegible] Endowment for Technical Education,	IV., 60
[illegible], Rev. [illegible], LL.D.,	Warden of St. Andrew's, [illegible]	IV., 191
[illegible]	One of the Governors of the Munster Dairy School,	IV., 31
[illegible], Rt. Rev. Monsignor, P.P., V.G.,	Manager of Schools, Parish Priest of Dungannon,	IV., 177
[illegible], Miss [illegible],	Hon. Secretary of the Liverpool Technical College for Women,	II., 163
[illegible]	One of Her Majesty's Inspectors of Schools in Scotland,	IV., 279
[illegible], Rev. [illegible], C.M.,	Vice-Principal, "St. Patrick's" Training College, Drumcondra,	IV., 340
[illegible], Rev. James, B.A.,	Presbyterian Minister, Londonderry,	IV., 134
[illegible], Thomas, [illegible]	Agricultural Superintendent, Albert Farm, Glasnevin,	I., 31; III., 80
[illegible], John,	Head Master, [illegible] School, Westmoreland,	II., 345
[illegible]	Presbyterian Minister, Belfast,	IV., 117

[illegible]	[illegible]
DALTON, J. P., M.A.,	District Inspector of National Schools,
DALY, Miss M.,	Professor of Kindergarten, &c., "Our Lady of Mercy" Tr[illegible] College, Dublin.
[illegible], J.,	National Teacher, [illegible] National School, Cork.
[illegible], E. P., M.A.,	District Inspector of National Schools,
[illegible], J. R., M.A.,	Member of the School Board for London,
[illegible], J. J., [illegible]	Professor and Principal, Training College, Marlborough [illegible] Dublin,
[illegible], Richard,	Chief of Inspection under the Board of National Education,
[illegible], M.,	National Teacher, [illegible] National School, Co. [illegible]
[illegible], W.,	National Teacher, [illegible] National School, Co. [illegible]
[illegible], [illegible],	Manual Instruction under the Glasgow School Board,
DuPort, Rev. C. D.,	One of Her Majesty's Chief Inspectors of Schools in Englan[illegible]
[illegible], P.,	Head Inspector of National Schools,
[illegible], Councillor,	Chairman of the Manual Instruction Committee, [illegible]
[illegible], G. R., M.A.,	Head Master, [illegible] School, Waterford,
[illegible], James,	Head Master, Model School, [illegible]
[illegible], Sir Joshua, M.A.,	Formerly One of Her Majesty's Chief Inspectors of [illegible] Colleges in England,
Fitzpatrick, [illegible],	Professor of Method, "St. Patrick's" Training College, Drum[illegible]
[illegible], [illegible],	National Teacher, [illegible] National School, Belfast,
[illegible], P. [illegible],	Professor of Drawing, "St. Patrick's" Training College, [illegible] [illegible],
[illegible], P.,	National Teacher, [illegible] National School, Cork,
[illegible], Wm. R.,	Treasurer to the Edinburgh School Board,
[illegible], [illegible],	Chairman of the Committee on Technical Education of the [illegible] Council,
[illegible], Rev. J., LL.D.,	Chairman of the [illegible] Agricultural Society, and [illegible]

ALPHABETICAL LIST OF WITNESSES—*continued*.

Name.	Description.
Kenny, Andrew D.,	National Teacher, [illegible] National School, [illegible], Galway,
Knight, Miss A. M.,	Organizing Teacher under the Board of National Education,
Kerr, John G., M.A.,	Head Master, Allan Glen's School, Glasgow,
Lally, Rev. P., P.P.,	St. Patrick's, Galway; Hon. Secretary, Galway Technical Sch[illegible]
Lavelle, E.,	National Teacher, [illegible] National School, [illegible]
Lawrence, W. T.,	Agricultural Instructor to the Cumberland County Council,
Legge, Joseph,	Manual Instructor to the Liverpool School Board,
Lord, Mrs.,	Organizing Superintendent of Laundry Work, &c., under School Board for London,
Low, Sir James,	Formerly Lord Provost of Dundee and Member of the [illegible] Instruction Committee, Dundee,
Lynskey, Very Rev. Canon, P.P., V.G.,	Manager of Schools: Parish Priest of Clifden,
McClelland, Miss M.,	Instructress in Cookery, "Our Lady of Mercy" Training Co[illegible]

ALPHABETICAL LIST OF WITNESSES—continued.

Name.	Description.	Volume and Page of Report
[illegible], H. R., M.A.,	Principal, University College, Bangor, North Wales,	III., 56
Robinson, George H.,	Head Master, [illegible] Board School, Birmingham,	II., 39
[illegible], T. [illegible],	One of Her Majesty's Inspectors of Schools in [illegible],	II., [illegible]
[illegible], James,	National Teacher, [illegible] National School, [illegible],	IV., [illegible]
Ryan, Rev. Patrick, P.P.,	Manager of Schools. Parish Priest, St. Joseph's, Berkeley-street, Dublin,	IV., [illegible]
Salomon, Herr Otto,	Director of the [illegible] Seminarium, [illegible], Sweden,	III., 100
[illegible], Andrew E., M.A., F.R.S.E.,	One of Her Majesty's Inspectors of Schools in Scotland,	IV., [illegible]
[illegible], J. B., M.A., LL.D.,	Head Inspector of National Schools,	IV., 6
[illegible], T. W.,	Director of Art and Manual Instruction to the Cumberland County Council,	II., 210
[illegible], D.,	District Inspector of National Schools,	IV., [illegible]
Somerville, William,	Professor of Agriculture and Forestry, Durham College of Science,	II., 218
[illegible], Rev. Dr.,	Rector of St. Mary's, [illegible], Dublin,	IV., 238
[illegible], Hon. Miss,	Hon. Secretary, [illegible] Branch, Irish Industrial Association,	IV., [illegible]
Stanley, Hon. E. Lyulph,	Member of the School Board for London,	II., [illegible]
[illegible], J., M.A.,	District Inspector of National Schools,	III., [illegible]
Stevenson, Miss Flora C.,	Member of the Edinburgh School Board,	IV., 501
[illegible], M.A.,	Head Inspector of National Schools,	I., 95; IV., 431
[illegible], [illegible] J.,	National Teacher, [illegible] National School, [illegible],	IV., 158
Tait, Andrew C.,	Head Master of [illegible] Training School, Edinburgh,	IV., [illegible]
[illegible], G. J.,	Head Master, [illegible] School, Dundee,	IV., [illegible]
[illegible], Richard H.,	Head Master, Birmingham Municipal School of Art,	II., 11
Taylor, John,	Head Master, [illegible] Board Schools, Birmingham,	II., 24
[illegible], W. H.,	Professor and Principal, Training College, Marlborough-street, Dublin,	IV., [illegible]
[illegible], Rev. Brother,	Principal, "De La Salle" Training College, Waterford,	IV., 1
Thomson, Miss Jane,	Infant Mistress, [illegible] Public School, Glasgow,	IV., [illegible]
[illegible], Archdeacon, [illegible],	Manager of Schools,	III., [illegible]
[illegible], Rev. J. W., D.D.,	Organising Secretary, Diocesan Board of Education, Dublin,	IV., [illegible]
Vaughan, Joseph,	Organising Teacher of Hand and Eye Training under the School Board for London,	II., [illegible]
Wallace, [illegible], F.E.I.S.,	Head Master, [illegible] Public School, [illegible], N.B.,	IV., [illegible]
Wallace, Robert,	Professor of Agriculture and Rural Economy in the University of Edinburgh,	IV., [illegible]
Ward, Philip,	National Teacher, St. [illegible] National Schools, Dublin,	IV., [illegible]
[illegible], W. H., B.A.,	District Inspector of National Schools,	IV., [illegible]
[illegible], Miss [illegible],	Hon. Secretary, Edinburgh School of Domestic Economy,	IV., [illegible]

LIST OF DOCUMENTS, RETURNS, AND OTHER PAPERS FURNISHED TO THE COMMISSION, AND PUBLISHED IN A SEPARATE VOLUME AS APPENDICES.

APPENDIX A.

DOCUMENTS.

I. Memorandum by the Commissioners of National Education on the subject of Manual Instruction.

II. Statement by His Grace the Most Rev. Dr. Walsh, on the subject of Manual Training.

III. Memorandum by Captain Shaw on Manual and Practical Instruction.

IV. Memorandum by Mr. Strachan on Manual and Practical Instruction.

V. Memorandum by Mr. M. E. Sadler on Manual Training for Boys in Primary Schools in Foreign Countries.

VI. Report by Mr. W. R. J. Molloy on a Visit to Harringay and Stroud Green Schools, Hornsey, London.

VII. Report by Mr. W. R. J. Molloy on a Visit to Abbey-street Schools, Bethnal Green, London.

VIII. Report on a Visit of some of the Commissioners to Westminster Training College, London.

IX. Documents put in by Mr. Alexander Hamilton, viz.:—

(1.) Subjects of Instruction in Irish National Schools.

(2.) Return showing Number and Size of School Rooms.

(3.) Return showing the operation of the Compulsory Attendance Act.

(4.) Revised Programme of Examination for Admission to Training Colleges.

(5.) Programme of Instruction and Examination in National Schools.

X. Documents put in by Professor Thomas Carroll, viz.:—

(1.) Return showing School Farms discontinued.

(2.) Prospectus of the Albert Agricultural Institution.

(3.) Return showing Number of Pupils who attended the Albert Agricultural Institution from 1881 to 1896.

(4.) Return showing the subsequent Occupations of Pupils who attended the Albert Agricultural Institution from 1881 to 1896.

(5.) Prospectus of the Munster Dairy School.

(6.) Return showing Number of Pupils who attended the Munster Dairy School from 1880 to 1896.

(7.) Lists of the following Classes of National Schools:—

(I.) Agricultural Training Establishments.

(II.) National Schools having School Farms.

(III.) National Schools having School Gardens.

(8.) Return showing Number of Pupils examined on School Farms and School Gardens.

(9.) Pamphlet on Agricultural Teaching under the Board of National Education.

XI. Memorandum by Miss Prendergast on the proposed Revision of the "Alternative Scheme."

XII. Memorandum by Miss A. M. Henry on the Extension of the Kindergarten system.

XIII. Memorandum by Miss M. Daly on the Extension of the Kindergarten System.

XIV. Letter by Mr. T. Healey on Sloyd and Kindergarten Occupations.

XV. Memorandum by Mr. T. Healey on a former System of Schools Teaching under the Board of National Education.

XVI. Memorandum by Mr. James Forbes on Dr. Clarke's Lectures on Physical Science.

XVII. Memorandum by Mr. A. W. Bone on the Case of Manual Training under the Birmingham School Board.

XVIII. Documents put in by Mr. W. Haydon Rolfe (School Board for London), viz.:—

(1.) "Circular R" of the Day School Code of the English Education Department.

(2.) Syllabus in Elementary Natural Philosophy.

(3.) Syllabus of a Course of Domestic Science.

LIST OF DOCUMENTS, RETURNS, &c.—continued.

XIX. Memorandum by Mr. J. Vaughan on Hand and Eye Training under the School Board for London.

XX. Memorandum by Mr. S. Barter on Drawing in connection with Manual Training.

XXI. Documents put in by Mrs. Hogan (School Board for London):—
- (1.) Scheme of Instruction in Cookery and Laundry Work under the School Board for London.
- (2.) Syllabus of Lessons in Cookery.
- (3.) Syllabus of Lessons in Laundry Work.

XXII. Documents put in by Mr. E. M. Hance (Liverpool School Board):—
- (1.) Particulars as to Certificates held by Instructors in Manual Work under the Liverpool School Board.
- (2.) Return showing subsequent Occupations of Students who received Manual Instruction in Liverpool.
- (3.) Return showing size of a Manual Instruction Centre recently erected in Liverpool.
- (4.) Return showing Cost of Manual Instruction under Liverpool School Board.

XXIII. Documents put in by Mr. A. T. Bass (Liverpool School Board):—
- (1.) Table showing Accommodation, &c. in the several Departments of the Liverpool Board Schools.
- (2.) Time Table for the Boys' Department in Brae-street School, Liverpool.
- (3.) Time Table for the Girls' Department in Brae-street School, Liverpool.

XXIV. Documents put in by Mr. J. Lomas (Liverpool School Board):—
- (1.) Syllabus of Lessons in Mechanics in Liverpool Board Schools.
- (2.) Syllabus of Lessons in Domestic Economy in Liverpool Board Schools.

XXV. Documents put in by Miss Fanny Calder (Liverpool Technical College for Women):—
- (1.) Syllabus of Twelve Laundry Lessons for Technical Classes.
- (2.) Syllabus of Twelve Lessons in Home Dress Cutting for Technical Classes.
- (3.) Syllabus of Ten Cookery Lessons given in Elementary Schools.
- (4.) Syllabus of Twelve Cookery Lessons given in Technical Classes.

XXVI. Documents put in by Mr. William Nelson (Manchester School Board):—
- (1.) Memorandum on Manual Instruction under the Manchester School Board.
- (2.) Courses in Manual Instruction under the Manchester School Board.
- (3.) Manual Instruction Time Table in Elementary Day Schools in Manchester.

XXVII. Prospectus of the Cumberland and Westmorland Farm School at Newton Rigg, Penrith.

XXVIII. Memorandum by Mr. J. Rider on the Cost of Manual Instruction.

XXIX. Memorandum put in by Dr. J. H. Gladstone—List of Apparatus for Object Teaching.

XXX. Documents put in by Mr. A. Hawkridge (Barrow-in-Furness School Board):—
- (1.) Scheme of Work for Infant Schools.
- (2.) Course of Nature Study.
- (3.) Notes on the Work of Infant Schools, &c.
- (4.) Course of Lessons in Cookery under the Barrow-in-Furness School Board.
- (5.) Course of Lessons in Laundry Work under the Barrow-in-Furness School Board.
- (6.) Woodworking Course for Standards V.–VII., under the Barrow-in-Furness School Board.
- (7.) Return showing Cost of Manual Instruction under the Barrow-in-Furness School Board.

XXXI. Memorandum by Mr. James Brenan, R.H.A., on the Instruction of National Teachers in the Dublin Metropolitan School of Art.

XXXII. Memorandum by Mr. H. Holland—Suggested Programme in Singing for National Schools.

XXXIII. Memorandum by Mr. Arnold Graves on Manual and Practical Instruction.

XXXIV. Memorandum by Miss M. M'Carthy—Suggested Programme of Cookery.

XXXV. Documents put in by Mrs. Power Lalor:—
- (1.) Suggestions and Remarks on the Programme of the Board of National Education.
- (2.) The People's Schools in Germany.

XXXVI. Document put in by Mr. W. T. Clements, Inspectors' Assistant.—Suggested Programme of Kindergarten and Manual Occupations.

LIST OF DOCUMENTS, RETURNS, &c.—*continued.*

XXXVII. Document put in by J. B. Skeffington, M.A., LL.D., District Inspector of National Schools.—Progressive Exercises in Kindergarten and Practical Instruction.

XXXVIII. Document put in by Mr. Richard H. Beamish, one of the Governors of the Munster Dairy School.—Memorandum on Agricultural Education in Sweden.

XXXIX. Document put in by Rev. Brother Gogarty, Instructor in Woodwork, Christian Brothers' Schools, Lismore.—Course of Manual Instruction in Wood at the Christian Brothers' Schools, Lismore.

XL. Document put in by Mr. J. P. Dalton, M.A., District Inspector of National Schools.—Suggested Programme in Elementary Science for National Schools.

XLI. Document put in by Mr. E. P. Dewar, M.A., District Inspector of National Schools.—Memorandum on Results Examinations in National Schools.

XLII. Document put in by Rev. Hugh M'Menamin, Adm., St. Columb's, Londonderry.—Memorandum on Evening Schools.

XLIII. Document put in by Rev. Edward M'Kenna, P.P., V.F., Claudy, Co. Londonderry.—Memorandum on Manual Instruction.

XLIV. Documents put in by Mr. William B. Gibson, Treasurer, Edinburgh School Board.—Cost of Equipment for Instruction in Woodwork.

XLV. Document put in by Mr. Andrew C. Tait, Head Master, Sciennes Evening School, Edinburgh.—Memorandum on Science in Evening Schools.

XLVI. Documents put in by Mr. Andrew E. Scougal, one of Her Majesty's Inspectors of Schools in Scotland:—

(1.) Cost of Manual Training, &c., under the Leith School Board.

(2.) Programme of Instruction in Lochend-road School, Leith:—

(a.) Kindergarten.

(b.) Manual Instruction.

(c.) Elementary Science.

(3.) Programme of Instruction in Couper-street Schools, Leith:—

(a.) Elementary Science.

(b.) Kindergarten.

(4.) Programme of Instruction in Woodwork in Newhaven Victoria School, Leith.

(5.) Programme of Instruction in Craighall-road School, Leith:—

(a.) Manual Instruction.

(b.) Kindergarten.

(c.) Cookery.

(d.) Elementary Science.

(6.) Programme of Instruction in Yardheads School, Leith:—

(a.) Elementary Science.

(b.) Kindergarten and Hand and Eye Training.

XLVII. Documents put in by Sir John Neilson Cuthbertson, Chairman of the School Board of Glasgow:—

(1.) Scheme of Object Lessons and Elementary Science Teaching for Standards I. to VI.

(2.) Regulations for Elementary Drawing.

XLVIII. Document put in by Mr. G. W. Alexander, M.A., Clerk to the School Board of Glasgow.—Cost of Apparatus for Elementary Science.

XLIX. Document put in by Mr. R. Calder, one of Her Majesty's Inspectors of Schools in Scotland.—Scheme of Science Teaching under the Dundee School Board.

L. Document put in by Mr. Stephen Fitzpatrick, Professor of Method, &c., St. Patrick's Training College, Drumcondra.—Suggested Programme of Examination for Entrance to Training Colleges.

LI. Documents put in by Professor Peyton, LL.B., Marlborough-street Training College, Dublin:—

(1.) Course of Elementary Drawing for Junior Classes.

(2.) Course of Object Lessons and Elementary Science.

(3.) Course of Lessons in Composition and Analysis of Sentences.

(4.) Suggestions for the Teaching of Practical Agriculture in National Schools.

LIST OF DOCUMENTS, RETURNS, &c.—*continued.*

[A Memorandum on Manual Instruction in Elementary Schools in Sweden, Russia, and Denmark, is published as an Appendix to the Third Volume of Evidence.]

APPENDIX B.

Reports of Assistants.

APPENDIX C.

Suggestions by Inspectors of Irish National Schools as to Modifications of the present Programme of Instruction in National Schools.

APPENDIX D.

French Scheme for teaching Elementary Ideas of Agriculture in Rural Schools.

APPENDIX E.

Digest of Minutes of Evidence.

APPENDIX F.

CHIEF SECRETARY'S OFFICE,

DUBLIN CASTLE,

29th June, 1898.

SIR,

I am directed by the Lords Justices to acknowledge the receipt of your Letter of the 27th instant, enclosing the final Report of the Commission on Manual and Practical Instruction in Primary Schools under the Board of National Education in Ireland.

I am,

Sir,

Your obedient Servant,

D. HARREL.

J. D. DALY, Esq.,

120, Lower Baggot-street,

Dublin.

www.ingramcontent.com/pod-product-compliance
Lightning Source LLC
Chambersburg PA
CBHW021528270326
41930CB00008B/1140